GEORGE
CRUIKSHANK:

THE ARTIST, THE HUMORIST, AND THE MAN,

WITH SOME ACCOUNT OF HIS BROTHER ROBERT.

𝕬 𝕮𝖗𝖎𝖙𝖎𝖈𝖔-𝕭𝖎𝖇𝖑𝖎𝖔𝖌𝖗𝖆𝖕𝖍𝖎𝖈𝖆𝖑 𝕰𝖘𝖘𝖆𝖞.

By WILLIAM BATES, B.A., M.R.C.S.E., ETC.,

Professor of Classics in Queen's College, Birmingham;
Surgeon to the Borough Hospital, etc.

WITH NUMEROUS ILLUSTRATIONS BY G. CRUIKSHANK
INCLUDING SEVERAL FROM ORIGINAL DRAWINGS
IN THE POSSESSION OF THE AUTHOR.

SECOND EDITION,

Revised ; and Augmented by a copiously Annotated Bibliographical Appendix, and
Additional Plates

AMSTERDAM
S. EMMERING
1972

" —————————————— quo fit ut omnis
Votivâ pateat veluti descripta tabellâ
Vita SENIS."

Horat ; SAT. *lib.* ii. 1.

" Men represent and describe according as they conceive, and they conceive
according to the frame of their imagination, and the turn of their opinions ;
so that among several persons, who have been spectators of the same thing,
we seldom meet with any two that report it in the same manner ; every one
describing what he has seen according to the ideas that he has formed
of it, according to the model of his own notions, and the texture of his own
intellect."

Rapin ; *Reflections on History.*

" 'Tis a thing of meere industry, a collection without wit or invention, a
very toy."

Burton ; *Anatomie of Melancholy.*

136271

Unchanged reprint of the original edition London 1879

ISBN 90 6033 171 0

Printed in The Netherlands

ANALYSIS OF CONTENTS.

LIST OF ILLUSTRATIONS.

* We are indebted for the use of this plate to the kindness of Messrs. Chatto and Windus, the publishers of "The Rose and Lily."

F. WENTWORTH, SC.

ACROSTIC.

GEORGE CRUIKSHANK—every heart, both young and old—
Even the middle, most uncertain, aged,
Owns satisfaction as thy name is told ;
Renown'd for long successful battle waged
'Gainst devils blue, that so in thraldom hold
English hearts, ever by themselves encaged.

CRUIKSHANK ! I do rejoice to see thy name
Reckon'd with Ainsworth's in the roll of fame !
Union most pregnant ! that with grace doth bind
In faithful bonds such pencil and such pen—
Kith bound to kin, and neither less than kind ;
So shall *young graces* bless us now and then.
Heaven marries truly such a mind and mind,
And shall command for both the hopes of men.
Now, trustful, let us forth with thee and Ainsworth,
Knowing full well it will be worth the pain's worth.

V. V., D.D.

—Ainsworth's Magazine,
June, 1842.

" Mrs. GAMP *loquitur.* " A gentleman with a large shirt collar, and a hook nose, and a eye like one of Mr. Sweedlepipes's hawks, and long locks of hair, and whiskers that I wouldn't have no lady as I was engaged to meet suddenly a turning round a corner for any sum of money you could offer me ——."
—Charles Dickens.

" George is popular among his associates. His face is an index of his mind. There is nothing anomalous about him and his doings. His appearance, his illustrations, his speeches, are all alike,—all picturesque, artistic, full of fun, feeling, geniality, and quaintness. His seriousness is grotesque, and his drollery is profound. He is the prince of living Caricaturists, and one of the best of men."
—Samuel Phillips.

" Few more interesting subjects could occupy a writer on art than the various and truly original genius of CRUIKSHANK."
—P. G. Hamerton.

GEORGE CRUIKSHANK.

I.

THIS country in her comparatively brief art-life has already produced four great typical masters of Pictorial Satire.

Purely national in genius; uninfluenced by school tradition or foreign example; devoting themselves to the honest exposition of the manners and doings of their time, the ridicule of its follies, and the castigation of its vices; each, in his special walk, seems to have reached the culminating point of graphic perfection; nor is it likely, so far as I can see, that even as time speeds on and judgment expands, other men will appear to surpass, or even equal these, as long as their own branch of art continues to be practised.

The earliest in point of time, WILLIAM HOGARTH, (1697-1764), took the entire drama of human life for the exercise of his pencil. Equally great in Tragedy and Comedy, he now lashes the sins of his age with the thong of Juvenal, and now ridicules its follies with the wit of Molière. The great "painter of mankind," we read his pictures as a book; he belongs, indeed, to literature as much as to art, and we often forget the painter in the author. His "pictured morals" raise him to the highest rank as an artist and as a teacher; and I am not aware that it has ever been doubted that he is the greatest didactic painter which this, or any other country, has, at any period, produced.*

---

* " Du onzième jusqu'à la fin du dix-huitième siècle, je constate de précieux monuments laissés par la caricature ; je ne vois pas le caricaturiste.

"Le peuple n'a pas encore choisi un défenseur hardi, en lui disant ; 'Tu seras roi.'

"Le premier roi fut un Anglais, un homme puissamment organisè, un peintre et un moraliste, Hogarth, le véritable père de la caricature qui, ce jour-là, élevée par un grand artiste, put inscrire le nom de son initiateur à côté de Fielding et de Swift.

"Cet homme de génie, dont les compositions compliquées appartiennent autant à la littérature qu' á la peinture ne trouva de successeur ni en Angleterre ni en France. Gillray, Rowlandson, les Cruikshank ne le firent pas oublier ; et en France Debucourt, Carl Vernet, Henry Monnier n'effleurèrent que des ridicules superficiels.—*Histoire de la Caricature Moderne* par Champfleury, p. xi.

The next in order of birth is THOMAS ROWLANDSON, (1756-1827). Of a reckless, jovial, happy disposition, he chose the broad Farce of social life for his field. With talents that might have raised him to the highest rank as an historical painter, or immortalised his name as a moral satirist, he was contented to remain a mere comic draughtsman. Degenerating into mannerism and extravagance, his unrestrained pencil sported with every imaginable scene of vice and folly, luxury and misery, sensuality and degradation. Yet he could draw the human figure with the strength of Mortimer and the grace of Stothard; could express more with little effort than almost any predecessor or contemporary; was a consummate master of composition; had the nicest eye for harmony of colour; and has produced designs, which, according to the judgment of Reynolds and West, would have done honour to Rubens, or any of the great masters of the old schools.

The third, JAMES GILLRAY, (1757-1815), was a genius of another order. Of an earnest and sombre turn of mind, his province may be termed the Tragedy of satire. The great master of graphic invective, he took the political life of his time for the subject of his art, and has drawn its history with all the virulent hate of Junius. He, like Rowlandson, might have taken a high place in historic art; was an admirable and most facile draughtsman; fertile in invention, powerful in design, and skilful in grouping; but, devoting himself exclusively to political satire, has simply left the name of the greatest of English—if not of modern—caricaturists.

We now come to GEORGE CRUIKSHANK, (1792-1878), the last of our quaternion,—if not of the line of purely comic artists,—the *omega*, as HOGARTH was the *alpha*, of satirical designers. Handing down the fire of national humour in direct descent from that great master, he, too, essayed the whole dramatic field; and thus a comparison is suggested, which, if pushed too far, is unfair to both. For the genius of the one differs from that of the other in kind as well as degree; and there is little resemblance in the circumstances of their lives. HOGARTH had the advantage of a thorough early training; CRUIKSHANK picked up his art when and how he could. The one has left us elaborate works, the results of deliberate thought and careful execution; the other, a vast number of trivial designs,

—" smiling offsprings of painful labour," as Thackeray finely calls them,—born of occasion and spontaneous impulse, redeemed and exalted alone by the informing art. HOGARTH rises higher in tragic power; CRUIKSHANK is more intensely comic. HOGARTH could draw a graceful figure, and has left us female faces of exceeding suavity and tenderness; CRUIKSHANK has no eye for æsthetic beauty, and is utterly mannered when he attempts to delineate the refinement of a gentleman, the elegance of a lady, or the simplicity of a child. In oils, HOGARTH had thoroughly mastered the technicalities of his art, was a fine colourist, and painted with the solidity of the old Dutch masters; while CRUIKSHANK is flimsy in texture, glaring in effect, and has no eye for chromatic harmony. But, if the later artist is inferior to the earlier when he comes in direct competition with him, he has reached the highest excellence in certain peculiar walks of his own. In the depiction of low, vicious, and vulgar life,—in the ludicrous, the quaint, the weird, the pathetic, and the terrible,—he is unsurpassed. No one has touched with a nicer humour the manners of his day, and the frivolities and affectations of fashionable life; no one so felicitously illustrated the mysteries of folk-lore and popular superstition. Like Hogarth, he possessed a supreme faculty of graphic narration, and an unerring tact in the seizure of dramatic incident. If occasionally incorrect in drawing, as much from the habitual license of the caricaturist as the want of early training, he shows the rare talent of preserving to every figure an individuality of its own, of fixing evanescent motion, and crowding his designs with life and action without confusion. As an etcher, if he cannot with justice be said to possess supreme mastery over the technical resources of the needle, he is simple and effective; uses no superfluous means; pervades his work with colour; and exhibits a command of light and shade only inferior to that of Rembrandt. Lastly, as a great moral teacher and satirist; as a castigator of our great national sin, and an illustrator by pen and pencil of its direful effects; he is entitled to the admiration and gratitude of our own and future times.

II.

Those who have a keen perception of Humour, and the faculty by pen, pencil, or mimic action, of exciting the humourous sensations of others, have generally a pathetic side of character, and some power of expressing or evoking tragic emotions. On the other hand, the grave, the dignified, the sententious, and the solemn among men do not necessarily possess the comic element, or any power of amusing at one time those whom they have instructed at another. Hence, I should be inclined to give an *a priori* pre-eminence to the comic artist, actor, or author; and believe him to be endowed with a wider range of intellect and sympathy. But to him who once dons it the garb of motley clings like the fatal tunic of Nessus. He must wear it through life and be content to excite laughter when he would fain evoke tears. The generality of men, however, find it difficult to respect where they laugh; or see in the comic artist any other qualities than those of the buffoon. The genius of HOGARTH met with but partial recognition, till the appearance of Charles Lamb's admirable essay. He it was who showed that to be a great artist, it was not necessary to paint great men, or "transactions over which time had thrown a grandeur;" that the amount of thought expressed, and the depth of interest excited, was, rather than the mere choice of subject, the measure of art; and that, consequently, an artist was not necessarily inferior or vulgar, because he took his subjects from common or vulgar life. The due appreciation of ROWLANDSON is yet to come. From their mere *vis comica,* his etchings and drawings have always found collectors; but as an artist, the world has been slow to recognise his higher merits. A comprehensive essay upon his life, times, and genius, long wanted, has been recently announced; and due justice may at length be done to his marvellous powers. GILLRAY, perhaps from his greater unity of purpose, and the more historical character of his work, is better known. Collections of his caricatures have been repeatedly published; and latterly, under such chronological arrangement, and so accompanied with illustrative commentary, as to furnish a perfect history of their political epoch.

With GEORGE CRUIKSHANK the case is altogether different. Covering by his art-life three-quarters of a century, our remote ancestors laughed at his comic humour; while our more immediate progenitors and ourselves, with that wider intelligence and appreciation, which Thackeray's generous article in the *Westminster*

Review (1840) did so much to quicken, had arrived at some truer perception of his higher qualities. Surviving himself in a certain sense, he had come to be regarded as an "old master," and saw collectors fighting over early scraps from his hand, the very existence of which he had himself forgotten. If the child, as Wordsworth has it, is the father of the man, he may well be held the grandfather of the septuagenarian; and so far back as 1863, the artist found it necessary to exhibit at Exeter Hall the continuous work of some sixty years, with the professed object of convincing a doubting generation that he did not stand in this relation to himself! The Catalogue set forth that this was "A Selection from the works of George Cruikshank, extending over a period of upwards of sixty years, from 1799 to 1863;" and that it comprised "upwards of one hundred oil-paintings, water-colour drawings, and original sketches, together with over a thousand proof etchings from popular works, caricatures, scrap-books, song-headings, &c., and the 'Worship of Bacchus.'" Lockhart in *Blackwood*, so early in the day as July, 1823, had told its readers that George Cruikshank was something more than a comic artist; and that it was time that they should think more of him, and that he should think more of himself.* Maginn, despite the "odium of his politics," in 1833 gave him a niche in Fraser's "Gallery of Illustrious Literary Characters."†

---

* See also "Noctes Ambrosianæ," No. xliv. Tickler (Sym.) *loquitur* :—"What a clever fellow George Cruikshank is. They said he was a mere caricaturist. Sir, he is a painter—a great painter." Lockhart's remarks, prefatory to his criticism upon the *Points of Humour*, are curious, and merit preservation. Referring to the artist, he says :—"He appears to be the most careless creature alive, as touching his reputation. He seems to have no plan—almost no ambition, and, I apprehend, not much industry. He does just what is suggested or thrown in his way—pockets the cash—orders his beef-steak and bowl—and chaunts, like one of his own heroes,

'Life is all a variorum,
We regard not how it goes.'

*   *   *   *   *   *   *   *   *   *

In the first place, he is—what no living caricaturist but himself has the least pretensions to be,—and what, indeed, scarcely one of their predecessors was—he is a thorough-bred *artist*. He draws with the ease, and freedom, and fearlessness of a master; he understands the figure completely; and appears, so far as one can guess from the trifling sort of things he has done, to have a capital notion of the principles of grouping. Now these things are valuable in themselves; but they are doubly, trebly valuable, as possessed by a person of real comic humour, and a total despiser of THAT VENERABLE HUMBUG, which almost all the artists of our day seem, in one shape or other, to revere as the prime God of their idolatry."—*Blackwood's Magazine*, July, 1823.

† The illustration here, drawn by the late Daniel Maclise, R.A., represents the artist seated on a beer-barrel, and making a sketch on the crown of his hat. "Here we have," writes Maginn, "the sketcher sketched; and, as is fit, he is sketched sketching. Here is George Cruikshank,—*the* George Cruikshank—seated upon the head of a barrel, catching

Walter Thornbury, in his *British Artists from Hogarth to Turner,* (2 vols., 1861, 8vo.,) gave him a special chapter, and hailed him "King of the Caricaturists." Dr. R. Shelton Mackenzie indited an appreciative "Essay" on his genius. Thomas Wright rounded off his admirable *History of Caricature and Grotesque in Literature and Art,* (1865), by a graceful tribute to the ability and character of his friend. Ruskin directed the attention of students to his etchings as an education in themselves, and the finest things in their way after Rembrandt.* W. M. Rossetti asserted, on behalf of the artist-world, that it was well recognized that his powers were not of the average, but the exceptional class; and that he was far from being one of those of whom each half-century repeats the type. Lastly, F. T. Palgrave, in his comments on the "Cruikshank Gallery," vindicated his claim to the title of a "great artist," and prophecied that Time, who had done justice to the author of the "Rake's Progress," had doubtless a like reparation in store for George Cruikshank.

Here, too, should be mentioned the splendid *Descriptive Catalogue* compiled by G. W. Reid, Keeper of the Prints in the British Museum, in which are recorded upwards of 5,000 separate productions, though the list does not go farther than 1870. Since the death of the artist, scores of critical notices have appeared in the public papers, all which—with Mr. Hamilton's published lecture, Mr. F. Wedmore's able article in the *Temple Bar*, Mr. G. A. Sala's genial "Life Memory" of his old friend in the *Gentleman's*, and

---

inspiration from the scenes presented to him in a pot-house, and consigning the ideas of the moment to immortality on the crown of his hat." George was not insensible to the honour conferred upon him, but nevertheless, in a letter to a friend, expressed "horror" at being so depicted. It doubtless seemed hard to one who was even then a Rechabite, that he should go down to posterity indebted for support to a beer-barrel, and able to pursue his graphic labours in the obnoxious propinquity of a tankard and a tobacco-pipe! But the artist had other grounds for objecting to the portrait, and these, as stated in a letter to myself, under date of April 30, 1873, are worthy of being placed on record. "I think it right to tell you," writes he, "that Maclise and I were friends, and that I held him in esteem as a worthy man and a great artist; but you will please to observe that the sketch which you allude to was made by him before we became acquainted, and is therefore not only not like me, but represents me doing what I never did in the whole course of my life,—that is *making a sketch of anyone.* All the characters which I have placed before the public are from the *brain*—after *studying and observing Nature*—and not from any sketches made on the spot."

* Referring to them, this distinguished critic remarks, "Nothing in modern line-work approaches these in pure, straightforward, unaffected rightness of method, utterly disdaining all accident scrawl, or tricks of biting."—*Notes on Turner's Drawings,* 1878, p. iii.

the illustrated article in *Scribner's Monthly*—are prefatory to the more extended study anticipated from the pen of Mr. Blanchard Jerrold, and the promised autobiography of the artist, edited by his respected widow and B. Ward Richardson, M.D., and now in the hands of Mr. Bell.

Awaiting these more substantive and exhaustive chronicles, I add another to the slighter essays of which I have spoken; basing what I have to say on my personal knowledge of the man,—what I have heard, read, or seen of his works—and the not inconsiderable collection of his productions in my own possession. Any thing of this kind,—of any kind, I am afraid, which is likely to appear,— must needs be imperfect; and will derive any value it may be found to possess from method of arrangement, individuality of opinion, and the record of facts and notice of works, omitted by former writers, either from choice, exiguity of space, or not having them under view when engaged upon their task.

III.

We all know that George Cruikshank, though of Scotch descent, was born in London, on September 27, 1792. Of his mother I know nothing, except that her name was Macnaughten, and her father had some employment of a maritime nature. Her husband, Isaac Cruikshank, was the son, as I have heard, of an impoverished Scotch gentleman, an adherent of the Pretender;* and who, thrown penniless upon his own resources after the disasters of '45, had per- force taken to art as a means of subsistence. Isaac was born, I believe, in Edinburgh, and being left early an orphan and destitute, also adopted art as a profession. Later on, he migrated southwards, and, establishing himself in London, doubtless had a " sair fecht " to support himself, his wife, a daughter, and two sons, Isaac Robert (born 1789), and George, the subject of this essay. With filial reverence, the latter describes him as " a clever designer, etcher, and engraver, and a first-rate water-colour draughtsman." We know that he was, at least, an artist of considerable talent in an humble walk of art, ready to turn his hand to anything that offered; now

---

* " All my ancestors," says George, " were mixed up in the Rebellion of '45." Letter to the *Times*, April 8, 1872.

Publish'd Mar. 1 1808 by LAURIE & WHITTLE, 53 Fleet Street London.

THE MULBERRY-TREE.

THE sweet brier grows in the merry green wood,
　　Where the musk-rose diffuses his perfume so free,
But the blight often seizes both blossom and bud,
　　While the mildew flies over the mulberry-tree.

In the nursery reared, like the young tender vine,
　　Mankind of all orders and ev'ry degree,
First crawl on the ground, then spring up like the pine,
　　And some branch and bear fruit like the mulberry-tree.

To the fair tree of knowledge some twine like a twig,
　　While some sappy sprouts with its fruit disagree;
For which we from birch now and then pluck a sprig,
　　Which is not quite so sweet as the mulberry-tree.

The vast tree of life we all eagerly climb,
　　And impatiently pant at its high top to be;
Though nine out of ten are lopp'd off in their prime,
　　And they drop like dead leaves from the mulberry-tree.

Some live by the leaf, and some live by the bough,
　　As the song or the dance their vocation may be;
And some live and thrive, though we know no more how
　　Than the dew that flies over the mulberry-tree.

But like weeping-willows we hang down the head,
　　When poor wither'd elders we're destin'd to be:
And we're minded no more than mere logs when we're dead,
　　Or the dew that flies over the mulberry-tree.

Yet like lignum vitæ we hearts of oak wear,
　　Or the cedar that keeps from the cankerworm free;
While the vine-juice we drain to dissolve ev'ry care,
　　Like the dew that flies over the mulberry-tree.

Published 1st March, 1808,

By LAURIE AND WHITTLE,

NO. 53, FLEET STREET, LONDON.

etching the comic designs of Woodward, now painting miniatures, with no small delicacy and character, and now drawing book-illustrations with much of the grace of his contemporary, the elder Corbould. He was an exhibitor at the Royal Academy in 1789, 90-92; and as a caricaturist, entered the lists against Gillray himself in defence of Pitt. George's first playthings were the needle and the dabber; but play insensibly merged into work as he began to assist his hard worked father. The earliest job in the way of etching for which he was employed and received payment was a child's lottery picture; this was in 1804, when he was about twelve years of age. In 1805 he made a sketch of Nelson's funeral Car, and a caricature etching of the "fashions" of the day. His earliest *signed* work is dated, I believe, two years later, and represents the demagogue Cobbett on his way to St. James's. His father's early death threw the lad on his own resources, and he quickly found that he must fight for a place in the world, as Fuseli told him he would have to do for a seat in the Academy. Any thing that offered was acceptable,—headings for songs,* and half-penny ballads, illustrations for chap-books, designs for nursery-tales, sheets of prints for children—a dozen on a sheet and a penny the lot,—vignettes for lottery-tickets, rude cuts for broadsides, political squibs,—"trivial fond records," now of the utmost rarity and value. Then came the "O.P." Riots for which he made some illustrations; but if these are of no better quality than the prose and verse satire recorded by Stockdale in his chronicle of this contemptible affair, (1810,) they can have nothing but their earliness and scarcity to give them value. But though George was thus born, as it were, with an etching point in his hand, the stage, rather than art, was the object of his youthful predilection. He often performed at juvenile theatres, and was received with such

---

* One of these now lying before me is a large etching, terribly out of drawing, but not altogether devoid of character and indication of future power, to illustrate a broadside song. It is entitled the "Mulberry Tree," and represents three gentlemen carousing beneath the branches of the tree which gives its name to the song, with a family seat in the hilly distance. On the left hand corner we read "Cruikshank, A.D., 1808;" and it is published by Laurie and Whittle, in the same year. The song closes with the verse:—

"Yet like liguum vitæ, we hearts of oak wear,
  Or the cedar that keeps from the canker-worm free;
While the vine-juice we drain to dissolve ev'ry care,
  Like the dew that flies over the Mulberry-tree."

applause both in comic and serious parts, as to cause him to think seriously of becoming an actor by profession.   Unwilling, however, to face the hardships of an itinerant career, he obtained an introduction to Mr. Raymond, the then manager of Drury Lane theatre, from whom he sought to obtain employment as a scene-painter, in the hope that this might eventually lead to the stage. In this capacity he is said to have painted a drop-scene, representing Sir William Curtis, the gastronomic alderman, (a favourite subject of his) looking over a bridge, so irresistibly ludicrous that it brought down the audience with roars of laughter.   But this employment, and that which began to flow in upon him at home, led to the abandonment of the idea which caused him to undertake it.   Otherwise he would doubtless have made an excellent actor ; he had much dramatic and mimetic talent ; and,—as in graphic art,—such versatility as to attempt with equal success the opposite parts of Glenalvon in *Douglas*, and the tailor in *Katherine and Petruchio*,—which latter character he once played at the Haymarket Theatre, for the benefit of a friend.   Some thirty years ago, I myself saw him admirably sustain the part of " Formal," in Ben Jonson's *Every Man in his Humour*, at an Amateur performance at the Theatre Royal, Liverpool, for the benefit of Leigh Hunt, and John Poole of " Paul Pry " celebrity.

But it is with the art-life of this extraordinary man that I have to do.   In attempting a review of this, which, if necessarily imperfect, shall yet have some pretensions to comprehensiveness and method, I shall prefer an analytical to a chronological arrangement, —or rather a combination of both.   By the term " caricature " I understand an exaggeration of distinguishing characteristics ; by " humour " one's own sense of the ridiculous and the power of awakening this in others.   Perhaps in the entire cycle of George Cruikshank's productions,—at all events far more generally than in those of Hogarth,—there is no single one in which some trace of these qualities is not to be found.   These terms therefore, as universally applicable, may be omitted ; and for all necessary purposes the entire work of the artist grouped under five distinctive headings ; viz. (I.) POLITICAL DESIGNS ; (II.) SKETCHES FROM SOCIAL LIFE ; (III.) ILLUSTRATIONS OF FICTION ; (IV.) THE SUPERNATURAL ; (V.) PAINTINGS IN OIL.

IV.

POLITICAL DESIGNS.—As a political caricaturist, Cruikshank was next in succession to Gillray himself, and one of his earliest tasks was to complete some of the plates left unfinished by that lurid genius, when, in 1811, he finally sank into mental imbecility.* Here Cruikshank was the inferior, and knew it. "I was not fit to hold a candle to Gillray," he has said. The men, indeed, differed as darkness from light. The one sombre, reserved, solitary, inscrutable, self-contained; the other genial, frank, simple, without one drop in his kindly nature of that *sæva indignatio* which the epitaph tells us ate into the heart of the Dean of St. Patrick's. Circumstances thrust the part of political caricaturist upon him, and he accepted it frankly, as he did all others. It was Napoleon Buonaparte in his fall and exile, and Frenchmen from the Londoner's traditional point of view,—cocked-hatted, spindle-shanked, with high cheek bones and shrugging shoulders,—that afforded the earliest subjects for his satiric pencil. As early as 1813, we have a large, coarsely executed, coloured etching, "Quadrupeds, or Little Boney's last Kick,"† and another, "Otium cum Dignitate, or a View of Elba"; and in 1815 a large and very spirited etching, full of bustle and movement, "Return of the Paris Diligence, or Boney rode over." In 1816, we find a marked improvement in refinement and style in "A swarm of English Bees hiving in the Imperial Carriage, &c."; and the next year gives us a coarser plate, "HUNT-ing the Bull," where we first get a glimpse of the Regent. Passing from these, and similar cartoons, all more or less in the manner of Gillray, we come to an important illustrated volume. This is *The Life of Napoleon, a Hudibrastic Poem in Fifteen Cantos, by Dr. Syntax*, 1817. The thirty coloured plates are equally coarse in sentiment and execution, and the verse mere doggrel; but the book is nevertheless a rare and covetable curiosity. This must not be confounded with W. H. Ireland's *Life of Napoleon*, published a few

---

* It is worthy of note that Cruikshank worked upon the very table which had previously belonged to Gillray. This interesting relic sold for £19 the other day, at the sale by Christie, of the artist's effects.

† There is another engraving bearing a similar title—"Quadrupeds, or the Manager's last Kick"—of which a copy may be seen in the Westminster Aquarium, (No. 31.) This is a skit upon the revival at the Adelphi in 1811 of Foote's play, "The Tailors, or a Tragedy for Warm Weather."

years later (1823-5) illustrated with twenty-three folded coloured etchings either from his own designs, or those of Isabey, Denon, Vernet, Girard, Swebach, &c., of which the editor states that "their execution could not have been placed in a more masterly hand than that of Mr. George Cruikshank."

Passing over with mere mention *The Scourge, or Monthly Expositor of Imposture and Folly,* for the ten volumes of which he produced thirty eight plates,—*The Meteor,* a rare serial,—and *The Loyalist's Magazine,* illustrating the "Rise, Reign, and Fall of the Caroline contest"—I come to one of the most important and admirable of his political caricatures. The subject of this was "Coriolanus addressing the Plebeians," and it was published in 1820. Here we have portraits of Dr. Watson the radical, Thistlewood the traitor, Carlile the Deist, Cobbett the demagogue, Hunt the "Orator," Wooler the "Yellow Dwarf," Cartwright the patriot, Thelwall the elocutionist, Hobhouse the liberal, Hone the publisher, and—himself. Passing from these, I must dwell at greater length upon the artist's connection with WILLIAM HONE, celebrated as a Parodist, Pamphleteer, and Antiquarian writer. This would commence early in the teens. Thus we have a very curious and rare portrait of "William Norris, an insane American, *rivetted alive in Iron,* and many Years confined in that state in BETHLEM. Sketched from the Life in Bethlem *(as he was seen there in 1815 by W. Hone)* and etched by *G. Cruikshank.*" In 1816 he etched a portrait of Stephen Macdaniel for Hone's curious *History of the Blood Conspiracy*; and we find his name attached to many a coloured print,† etching for broad-side ballad, or wood-cut vignette for political pamphlet, ‡ issued by the same restless spirit. § In 1819 appeared that remarkable series of

† The following important etchings may be mentioned, "The King's Statue at Guildhall, or French Colours and French Principles put down, a serio-comic Dialogue," published at two shillings; "The Royal Shambles, or the Progress of Legitimacy, and Re-establishment of Religion and Social Order," 3s.; "Louis XVIII, climbing the Mât de Cocagne, or Soaped Pole, to bear off the Imperial Crown," 2s.; and "Fast Colours—Patience on a Monument Smiling at Grief, or the Royal Laundress Washing Boney's Court Dresses," 1s.

‡ Such as Hone's reprint of the fervid and eloquent *Spirit of Despotism* of Dr. Vicesimus Knox, 1821; the *Official Account of the Noble Lord's Bite;* the *Trial of the Dog for Biting the Noble Lord,* &c.

§ One of this kind which might be read with interest at the present day is entitled : "Bags Nodle's Feast; or the Partition and Re-union of Turkey! a new Ballad founded on Fact." —W. Hone, **1817,** a folio sheet with two large etchings, published at 2s., now worth as many guineas.

political squibs by the illustrations to which—rude as some of them were—his reputation as the first comic draughtsman of the day was firmly established with the public. Among these may be mentioned *The Political House that Jack Built, The Frown from the Crown, The Man in the Moon, The Green Bag, Doll Tearsheet, The Christmas Carol, The Queen's Matrimonial Ladder, Non mi Ricordo, Nero Vindicated, The Political Showman at Home, The Right Divine of Kings to Govern Wrong, The Slap at Slop,* and a number of others. In these celebrated pamphlets a profligate Prince and an obnoxious Ministry were bespattered with a pitiless shower of abuse and ridicule. As Gillray with remorseless thong had scourged the King, Sheridan, Burke, Canning and Pitt, so now Cruikshank, with more playful but yet cutting lash, castigated the Regent, Castlereagh, Sidmouth, Wellington and Copley. But it is the Regent, the poor plethoric Prince,—

> "The Dandy of Sixty, Who bows with a grace,
> And has taste in wigs, Collars, cuirasses and lace,"—

who is pilloried on every page for public execration and contempt,

—now astride on Sidmouth's back, taking aim at liberty with a

blunderbuss,—now maudlin in his cups,—hiding his face with shame, as prodigal son before the old king,—sawing off a beam on which he is seated, between himself and the wall,—doing penance in a sheet,—frizzling on a grid-iron, as "the fat in the fire !—or prostrate at the foot of the matrimonial ladder,—

> " Be warn'd by his fate, married, single and all ;
> Ye elderly gentlemen, pity his fall ! " *

With *The Queen's Matrimonial Ladder*, should be secured, if possible, the too often eliminated "Toy,"—the representation of a Ladder, printed on card-board, in two columns, the rungs bearing significant legends, and in the interspaces, in white on a black ground, a series of fourteen exquisitely drawn episodes in the short married life of George and Caroline.

In 1820, from the 11th to the 15th November, there was a public illumination, " to celebrate the victory obtained by the Press for the Liberties of the People, which had been assailed in the person of the Queen." On this occasion, George painted for Hone's shop-front an appropriate symbolical "Transparency," with the words " TRIUMPH OF THE PRESS " displayed in variegated lamps, as a motto above it. This Transparency was once more exhibited on November 29th, when the Queen went to St. Paul's. An engraving of it is given in the *Political Showman.*

Again, in 1822, we have the very curious etched and coloured frontispiece to Fairburn's *Kilts and Philibegs; The Northern Excursion of Geordie, Emperor of Gotham, and Sir Willie Curt-His, the Court Buffoon, &c., a Serio-Tragico-Comico-Ludicro-Aquatico Burlesque Gallimaufry, interspersed with Humourous Glees, Sporting Catches and Rum Chaunts by the Male and Female Characters of the Piece;* and, again ridiculing the Prince and the Alderman, a coloured etching, inscribed, " Turtle Doves and Turtle Soup ! or,

---

* I am aware that it is considered the right thing at the present day to lavish every epithet of abuse upon the unfortunate Regent. Thackeray set the fashion and the *imitatorum servum pecus* follow the bell-wether. Thus Mr. Hamilton tells us that " his life was as false, cruel, and useless, as his death was shameful, lingering and agonising." Now I am not the defender of the character of the Prince, so will not question the truth of the statement as far as it regards his *life*; but I am curious to know the authority for that which concerns his *death*. The primary cause of this, as certified by the surgeons who conducted the *post-mortem* examination—Messrs. Halford, Tierney, Astley Cooper and Brodie —was an ossification of the valves of the *aorta*, of many years standing. This led, as usual, to dropsy, and the other symptoms manifested ; but the more immediate cause was the rupture of a blood vessel in the stomach. The death was "lingering" and " agonizing," I know ; but I quite fail to see that it was " shameful."

a Try-O between Geordie, a Northern Lassie, and Sir Willey O ! ! "
" We Tory folk," says Maginn, " were terribly angry at the time,
but we soon confessed that the caricaturist was a clever fellow."
This comes well from the " Doctor," who was writing at the same
time leaders for the *Age*, the ultra Tory paper, and for the *True Sun*,
a print as outrageously radical ! But the fact is George was no
politician, and would make a design with rigid impartiality for any
one that paid him. Thus, in 1819—at the very time that he was
employed by Hone, an ultra Radical, or just before it—he produced
a remarkable etched design (14-in. by 10-in.) " Death or Liberty !
or Britannia and the Virtues of the Constitution in danger of
Violation from the great Political Libertine, Radical Reform ! "
where we see Britannia seized by a Republican demon, followed by
a train of attendant imps wearing the Phrygian caps of Liberty. He
etched the capital coloured front for *The Radical Ladder, or Hone's
Political Ladder and his Non Mi Ricordo explained and applied ;*
and that for the *Loyal Investigation and Radical Non Mi
Ricordo*—both published in 1820 at the expense of the Loyal
Association. He also produced the spirited full-page etching,
" The Mother Red-Cap Public House in opposition to the King's
Head," to serve as front to a loyal pamphlet: *The Royal Wanderer
Beguiled abroad and Reclaimed at Home ; or a Sketch of St.
Caroline's Pilgrimage to the Holy Land, &c.* (W. Wright, 1820,
8vo) ; and in the following year he was illustrating *The Loyalist ;
or Anti-Radical*, published in weekly parts, also at the expense of
the Loyal Association.

But though thus freely airing his loyalty, his instincts certainly
rather led him to the other side. He was essentially a man of the
people, and so naturally took the popular view. He saw that the
poor were oppressed and eaten up by taxes ; and he had a strong
idea that an innocent woman was insulted and outraged. Hence the
manliness and chivalry of his nature were called forth. Besides
this he was actuated by a warm friendship for Hone, who was
anything but the despicable character it is the fashion to represent
him. Every form of abuse has been lavished upon this poor
wight. The *Quarterly Review* stigmatized him as " a wretch as
contemptible as he is wicked," and informed its readers that he was
' a poor illiterate creature." Then we are told that the text of the

pamphlets is utter trash, that the caricaturist made his fortune,
(poor Hone, his "fortune!"), that he paid him little for his help
or that he paid him nothing at all. All this is false. The friend
of Charles Lamb and Barry Cornwall can hardly have been a
worthless or ignorant man ; the squibs are smart and telling,—and
one, *The Political Showman at Home,* is, though a mere *cento,* put
together with rare skill, and is one of the most curious pamphlets
I happen to know. Then, as to payment, it is possible that Hone's
profits and Cruikshank's remuneration have been alike mistated.
Any way, Hone was and remained a poor man, and died in utter
poverty ; and the artist, as I can testify from my own conversations
with him, though certainly speaking of the exiguity of his receipts,
made no complaint. It was manifestly the interest of Hone to keep
him content, and he doubtless paid the artist more than others had
done. As a bitter contemporary satirist says :—

> " I grant exceptions sometimes may occur ;
> 　　For instance, such dull boggling slang as *you* sell,
> However coarse, attention would not stir,
> 　　Nor barrow-women of their pence bamboozle,
> Without a wood-cut to explain the sense,
> And help along its lame incompetence.
>
> Therefore the wisest job that ever you did,
> 　　(Next to your well-known trial and subscription)
> Was your flash bargain with a wag concluded,
> 　　To aid your thread-bare talent for description.
> For who, in fits at Cruiky's droll designs,
> Can stay to criticize lop-sided rhymes ;
>
> Make much of that droll dog and feed him fat ;
> 　　Your gains would fall off sadly in amount,
> Should he once think your letter-press too flat,
> 　　And take to writing on his own account.
> Your libels then would sell about as quick, Sir,
> As bare quack labels would without th' elixir.
>
> 　*　　*　　*　　*　　*　　*　　*
> 　　*　　*　　*　　*　　*　　*　　*
> *　　*　　*　　*　　*　　*　　*
> 　　*　　*　　*　　*　　*　　*　　*
>
> Were Cruikshank wise, he might with trouble small,
> Write his own labels, and eclipse you all.

And thus short-sighted to his own full merit,
　He much reminds me of the fabled blind ;
So pay his pencil, Master H—e, with spirit,
　Humour and keep him still in the same mind.
And drive not the hard bargain, which, as I know,
You schemers do with wags who get your rhino "

Slop's Shave at a broken Hone, 1820, page 11.

However the pecuniary account stood between author and artist, their mutual esteem continued to subsist after a lull in political excitement had brought the "pamphlets" to a close.* In 1822, the latter made a capital design,—a double execution by axe and by halter, full of gloomy horror,—for Cecil's *Sixty Curious and Authentic Narratives,* published by Hone. In the same year we have a very curious pamphlet, *The Miraculous Host tortured by the Jew, under the Reign of Philip the Fair, 1290, being one of the Legends which converted the Daughters and Niece of Douglas Loveday, Esq., under the reign of Louis XVIII., in 1812. From the original French work, authorised by the College of Theology at Paris, in the Publisher's possession,*† (William Hone, 1822, 8vo., pp. 32). Here we have nine cuts drawn by G. C., from the same number of designs in the original volume, to illustrate one of those absurd and lying fables, which told for centuries in a hundred different ways, are a disgrace alike to human nature and religion In 1823 he produced some excellent antiquarian designs for Hone's curious work, *Ancient Mysteries described, especially the English Miracle Plays founded on Apocryphal New Testament Story.* Here we have a capital coloured plate,—"drawn and etched from the Statues"—of Corinœus and Gog-Magog, the Giants in Guildhall, respecting which the author says :—

"In order to perpetuate their appearance, they are drawn and etched by Mr. George Cruikshank, whose extraordinary talents have been happily exercised on my more original fancies. As this may be the last time I shall ever write Mr. Cruikshank's name for the press, I cannot but express my astonishment that a pencil which commands the admiration of every person

---

* It is much to be regretted that the *Complete History of Parody* announced by Hone in 1820, as in preparation, was never given to the world. It was to have "extensive graphic illustrations ; " and these, it may well be imagined, would have afforded as happy an exercise for the artist's pencil, as the "History" itself for the farther display of the learning, courage and sagacity which the Parodist had manifested on the memorable occasion of his "Three Trials" before Mr. Justice Abbott and Lord Ellenborough in 1817.

† The title of the original work is *L'Histoire de l'Hostie Miraculeuse arrivée au Couvent des Religieux Carmes du Saint Sacrement des Billetes,* par Fr. Leon, Paris, 1664, 12mo., pp. 274.

qualified to appreciate art, should be disregarded by that class, whose omission to secure it in their service is a remarkable instance of disregard to their own interests as the midwives of literature."—Page 276.

Later on, in 1826, when Hone sought, by the publication of his well-known *Every Day Book*, to popularise his vast stores of curious and antiquarian information, Cruikshank furnished him with eleven designs. They are, however, somewhat careless in drawing and coarse in execution, contrasting ill with the symbolical representations of the months in the following *Table Book*, drawn and engraved by that admirable artist, the late Samuel Williams. A year later, in 1827, Hone collected together a few complete sets of his pamphlets, and issued them under the general title of *Facetiæ and Miscellanies. By William Hone. With one hundred and twenty Engravings drawn by George Cruikshank*,—a volume now of considerable rarity, and which I regard as perhaps the most interesting and permanently valuable in the whole cycle of *Cruikshankiana*. A vignette on the title-page gives us capital portraits of author and artist* confabulating over a table, with the epigraph from Burns, "We twa hae paidl't":—just as, long years after, a plate in *Ainsworth's Magazine*, styled "Our Library Table," shows Cruikshank and the editor in literary consultation, and another in the *Sketches by Boz*, exhibits the artist and Dickens as managers of a Charity dinner; all this manifesting a fondness for giving the world his own portrait,—he said it was done at the request of publishers—which characterised him throughout.

Besides this, we have another pleasing record of the friendship which existed between Hone and Cruikshank, in a note to one of the controversial tracts appended to the volume. Here the author takes occasion to speak with honest pride of what he has done for popular art, and pays a grateful tribute to the merits of his friend :—

"The pieces I brought out with which the public are best acquainted, were the products of my own pen. Be their merits or demerits what they may, one real service has resulted from them. By showing what engraving on wood could effect in a popular way, and exciting a taste for art in the more humble ranks of life, they created a new era in the history of publication. They are the parents of the present cheap literature, which extends to a sale

---

* I have before me a portrait of William Hone, engraved in the stipple manner by Rogers, from a drawing by George Cruikshank.

of at least four hundred thousand copies every week, and gives large and constant employment to talent in that particular branch of engraving, which I selected as the best adapted to enforce and give circulation to my own thoughts.

"Besides this, I have the high satisfaction of knowing that my little pieces acquainted every rank of society, in the most remote corner of the British dominions, with the powers of MR. GEORGE CRUIKSHANK, whose genius had been wasted on mere caricature, till it embodied my ideas and feelings. When his brother artists, and everyone who had the least judgment, praised the multiform fertility of the freest pencil that ever drew a line on a block, it began to be appreciated by publishers. His recent designs in that way, though some have been cruelly cut up by unskilful or careless wood engravers and his own excellent etchings, with the currency they give to the works they appear in, incontestibly prove that his abilities have forced themselves into demand. His conception of original fancy seems intuitive, and yet his elaboration of a fac-simile would glisten the peering eye of a bibliomaniac. I barely do justice to his talents by this remark; and I have more satisfactory evidence of its truth than a certificate 'with five justices' hands to it, and witnesses more than a page could hold.' Robert Burns had not more kindly feelings when he wrote *Auld Lang Syne*, than I have towards my friend George Cruikshank. 'We twa ha' paddled'; and though as regards me, his occupation's gone, our mutual esteem is undiminished. Those who require his assistance may consider this a note of introduction to him, at his house, No. 25, Middleton Terrace, Pentonville."—*Aspersions Answered*, page 49.

Some dozen years ago, I read this passage, which I do not think has been cited before, and is certainly too curious to be forgotten, to the artist; but it seemed quite strange to him, and it was evident that no one had ever used it as "a note of introduction." That the regard, so gracefully expressed, was reciprocal, no further evidence is required to show than George's courageous vindication of his early associate, when accused, a score of years later, of having been on "terms of warm friendship with the most noted infidel of the day ":—

"What Mr. Hone's religious creed may have been at that time, I am far from being able to decide; I was too young to know more than that he seemed deeply read in theological questions, and although unsettled in his opinions, always professed to be a Christian. I knew also that his conduct was regulated by the strictest morality. He had been brought up to detest the Church of Rome, and to look upon the Church of England service as little better than Popish ceremonies; and with this feeling he parodied some portions of the Church service for purposes of political satire. But with their publication I had nothing whatever to do; and the instant I heard of their appearance, I entreated him to withdraw them. That I was his friend, it is true; and it is true also that among his friends were many persons, not more admired for their literary genius, than esteemed for their zeal in behalf of religion and morals."   *The Omnibus*, page 3.

I have seen the hieroglyphic cuts that adorn *Poor Humphrey's Calendar,*—an Almanack for the year 1829, written by Hone and published by his daughter, Matilda, who had commenced business as a print-seller in Russell Court—attributed to Cruikshank, but I am quite sure they are not from his hand.

Poor Hone, who had failed successively as bookseller, publisher, and author, made a last adventure as eating-house keeper in Grace-church Street. This failed too, and his troubled career closed in utter poverty, on Nov. 6, 1843. Cruikshank attended the funeral in company with Charles Dickens; and here the warm-hearted artist was once more fain to take up the cudgels in defence of his friend. The service was conducted by an Independent minister, who thought fit to give utterance to some disparaging remarks upon the religious character of the defunct. At this Cruikshank was so greatly incensed that he whispered to his companion, in a voice broken by sobs,—*teste* Forster,—that, " if it wasn't a clergy-man,—and if it wasn't a funeral,—he'd punch his head ! "

One plate included among Hone's *Facetiæ* must have something more than a passing notice, inasmuch as its production was con-sidered by the artist " the great event of his artistic life," and upon it, as a successful effort in the cause of humanity, he ever looked back with the liveliest satisfaction. The story has often been told, and by himself too. How, passing Newgate on his way to the Royal Exchange, in 1818, he saw dangling from the gallows a row of unfortunates, among whom were two women, convicted of passing one-pound forged notes ; how, with the terrible sight in his memory, on his return home, he drew and etched his " Bank Restriction Note—Not to be Imitated," signed by Jack Ketch, and symbolically adorned with fetter, halter, and gibbet ; how Hone dropping in, saw the design,—" What's this," says he,—" George, you must let me have this ; " how the next thing the careless artist heard of his work was that the Lord Mayor had had to send the constabulary to clear away the crowd from Hone's window in Ludgate Hill ; how the " Notes " could not be printed fast enough to satisfy the demand at a shilling each, and how George had to sit up all night to etch another plate ; and finally how Hone cleared £700 by the sale, and the artist,—" the satisfaction of knowing

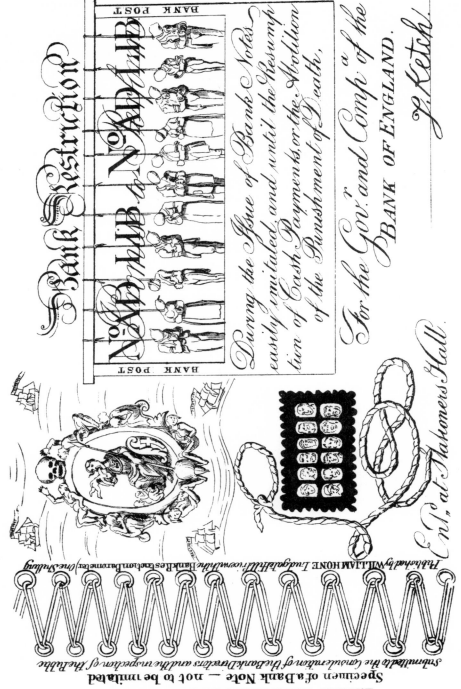

Bank Restriction

No. —— BLLLLLIP to BLLLLLIP

During the Issue of Bank Notes
easily imitated, and until the Resump-
tion of Cash Payments, or the Abolition
of the Punishment of Death.

For the Gov.ʳ and Comp.ᵃ of the
BANK OF ENGLAND.

J. Ketch.

Published by WILLIAM HONE Ludgate Hill three white Bank Restriction Barometers) one Shilling

Ent.ᵈ at Stationers Hall.

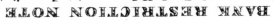

BANK RESTRICTION NOTE
Specimen of a Bank Note — not to be imitated
Submitted to the Consideration of the Bank Directors and the inspection of the Public

THE

BANK RESTRICTION BAROMETER;

OR, SCALE OF EFFECTS ON SOCIETY OF THE

Bank Note System, and Payments in Gold.

BY ABRAHAM FRANKLIN.

⁎ *To be read from the words* "BANK RESTRICTION,' *in the middle, upwards or downwards.*

NATIONAL PROSPERITY PROMOTED.

10. The Number of useless Public Executions diminished.

9. The Amelioration of the Criminal Code facilitated.

8. The Forgery of Bank Notes at an end.

7. Manufacturers and Journeymen obtain Necessaries and Comforts for their Wages.

6. The Means of Persons with small Incomes enlarged.

5. A Fall of Rents and Prices.

4. The Circulating Medium diminished.

3. Fictitious Capital and False Credit destroyed.

2. Exchanges equalized, and the Gold Coin preserved, if allowed to be freely exported.

1. The Gold Currency restored.

Consequences, if taken off, will be as above :—viz.

THE BANK RESTRICTION.

Consequences of its Operation are as follows :—viz.

1. Disappearance of the legal Gold Coin.

2. The Issues of Bank of England Notes and Country Bank Notes extended.

3. Paper Accommodation, creating False Credit, Fictitious Capital, Mischievous Speculation.

4. The Circulating Medium enormously enlarged.

5. Rents and Prices of Articles of the first Necessity, doubled and trebled.

6. The Income and Wages of small Annuitants, and Artisans and Labourers, insufficient to purchase Necessaries for their Support.

7. Industry reduced to Indigence, broken-spirited, and in the Workhouse : or, endeavouring to preserve independence, lingering in despair, committing suicide, or dying broken-hearted.

8. The Temptation to forge Bank of England Notes increased and facilitated.

9. New and sanguinary Laws against Forgery ineffectually enacted.

10. Frequent and useless inflictions of the barbarous Punishment of Death.

GENERAL DISTRESS INCREASED.

that no man or woman was ever hanged after this for passing one pound forged Bank of England notes." The Directors of the Bank of England, George tells us, were "exceedingly wroth."

Among the political pamphlets of the day, is one entitled, "*Who Killed Cock Robin? a Satirical Tragedy, or Hieroglyphic Prophecy on the Manchester Blot ! ! !* (London, 1819). This is illustrated by the veteran caricaturist, Thomas Rowlandson, by etchings on copper, of which that on page 4, representing the yeomanry heroes of Peterloo cutting down the "Manchester Robins," is a spirited and admirable, if mannered, production of his needle. Now Rowlandson was a strapping lad of eight at the death of Hogarth; he was an associate of Gillray; and here we have him working side by side, as it were, with an artist who but the other day was living and sketching in our midst! *Vidi tantum;* there may not be much in the boast, but it certainly awakens curious feelings in the mind, to reflect that one has conversed with an artist who was once on friendly terms with a "brother of the brush," who might possibly have seen in the flesh the great father of pictorial satire!

Here may be said to close the artist's brief career as a political caricaturist. He had too little gall in his composition to devote himself permanently to a branch of art which has the fatal defect of never seeking beauty, and always exaggerating defect. He had now gained fame; and was known alike to public and publishers. More congenial employment came in to divert his talents into a different channel; nor am I aware that even the political excitement of the year preceding and following the passing of the Reform Bill of 1832, produced anything of note from his hand.

V.

Sketches from Social Life.—The earliest plate of any importance to which this description applies, which occurs to me, is the capital folding frontispiece to *Metropolitan Grievances*, (1812), a humorous exposition of London street nuisances. This etching is full of broad humour, much in the manner of Rowlandson; and so is another, published in the same year by G. Humphrey, entitled, *The Cholic.* In 1817, Mr. Roberts published *The State Lottery, a Dream,* accompanied by the *Thoughts on Wheels* of James Montgomery. "Its frontispiece," says the latter, in allusion to George's very curious contribution to the work, "representing *A Petty State Lottery* within the walls of Christ's Hospital, in which not the drawers only,' but all the adventurers, were children of that venerable establishment, was not without its effect in abating one of the most plausible but pernicious exhibitions at Guildhall and elsewhere, in the annual pantomime of *The Grand State Lottery.*"

A plate which had appeared in 1813, "A Sparring Match at the Fives Court," etched by George from a design by his brother, Isaac Robert, and illustrating No. 13 of the original issue of *Boxiana,* published by Smeeton, is worthy of note as the conjoint work of the brothers, and indicating the early connection between them and "Fancy's child," the once celebrated Pierce Egan. It was not, however, till 1821, that this gentleman, alluded to, I know not with what justice, by Grantley Berkeley in his *Reminiscences,* as "rather a low-caste Irishman," and who ended his long career some thirty years ago, almost an octogenarian*, gave to an admiring world his famous *Life in London; or, the Day and Night Scenes of Jerry Hawthorn, Esq., and his elegant friend, Corinthian Tom, accompanied by Bob Logic, the Oxonian, in their Rambles and Sprees through the Metropolis.* This work was embellished with thirty-six "scenes from life," designed and etched by I. R. and G. Cruikshank, and many very clever designs on wood by the same artists. The story is, as he has often related it to myself and others, that George, who was even then a moralist, either had misconceived the object of the author, or saw that his designs were used for a purpose he had not contemplated; and finding that the book, which created a perfect *furore,* was a guide to, rather than a dissuasive from, the vicious haunts and amusements of the metropolis, retired from the firm, in which, from relative age, he figured as junior partner. Certain it is that the greater part of the work was done by the elder brother,—the plates throughout, some of which were of great excellence, showing unmistakeable traces of his

---

*Pierce Egan died August 3, 1849, aged 77 years. The only account of this once famous personage known to me will be found in the matter prefatory to the late J. C. Hotten's reprint of *The Finish.* Odoherty, in the "Noctes," (*Blackwood's Magazine,* March, 1822), says, "Egan is a prime swell." His son, "Pierce Egan, junior," well known as an artist and author, is still living at Ravensbourne, Kent. Among his works may be mentioned *The Pilgrims of the Thames in search of the National,* both written and illustrated by himself.

style. What, for instance, can be better in their way than the bustle and animation of the "Pinks in Rotten Row,"—the Hogarthian humour of the monkey and dog fight in the Westminster Pit,—or the suave contours of the couple who sport the light fantastic toe at Corinthian Kate's? The text I will not pretend to criticise; merit of some kind must be conceded to it, if only that of exactly hitting the taste of the day; and the book attained a popularity only equalled, on grounds to us more obvious, by the works of Dickens at a later date. It was dramatized by Jerrold, Barrymore, and the Dibdins; by the author himself for Covent Garden; and by Moncrieff for the Adelphi, under the management of Yates, where it had a run of 300 nights. It was pirated and imitated in various forms; balladized; translated into French; turned into "a Whimsical and Equestrian Drama" for Davies's Royal Amphitheatre, and a "*Mill*-Dramatic Burletta" for the Surrey. The "Rambles and Sprees" of Tom and Jerry were depicted on tea-boards,—"the laughable phiz of the Eccentric Bob Logic" grinned on snuff-box lids,—while the actors of the parts,—Mr. Russell and Pierce Egan as "Bob Logic," Oxberry and Reeves as "Jerry," and Wrench as "Corinthian Tom," (the prototype of whom was said to be the Marquis of Worcester, afterwards Duke of Beaufort)—were handed down to posterity by engravings.

Ten years later, Pierce Egan published the "Finish" to his immortal work, a volume of the same size as its predecessor, and illustrated by an equal number of coloured plates, this time all by the elder brother, Isaac Robert. In this latter volume the story is rounded off with fit poetic justice, according to the author's view. Corinthian Kate makes a melancholy end; the surnameless Tom breaks his neck, fox-hunting; Bob Logic gets his *quietus* from Dr. Finish'em; and the book ends with "all happiness at Hawthorn Hall, and the Nuptials of Jerry and Mary Rosebud." It is a little curious perhaps that, as pointed out by Mr. Hotten in his reprint, there is some similarity between the scenes and characters in this book and those of the immortal *Pickwick Papers*. In the former we have the *Bench*, in the latter the *Fleet*; in the one the *Archery Meeting*, in the other the *Shooting Party*; the "fat Knight" may be held to adumbrate the hero of Dickens ; and it is certainly a singular coincidence that it was at a place bearing the suggestive title of "Pickwick" that Corinthian Tom first met Sir John Blubber.   Both the *Life* and the *Finish* are, in the original issues, sufficiently rare ; and though a more squeamish generation relegates them to an upper shelf, they are well worthy of preservation and remembrance as a picture of manners, and a record of the taste and manners of their day. ·

One of the numerous imitations must have a special record. This is David Carey's *Life in Paris, comprising the Rambles, Sprees and Amours of Dick Wildfire of Corinthian celebrity, and his Bang-up companions, Squire Jenkins and Captain O'Shuffleton, with the whimsical Adventures of the Halibut Family, &c.* (London, Fairburn, 1822.) This volume contains twenty-one coloured plates, all by George Cruikshank, "representing scenes from real life." Hogarth had visited Paris which he admirably characterised, though in words that will not now bear reproduction ; but I am not aware that Cruikshank ever saw the French capital, so that he must have evolved the "real life," in part at least, from his inner consciousness.   However this may be, the plates are characteristic, cleverly drawn, and well coloured.   A year or two before, he had drawn the folding front for his friend Hone's curious *Picture of the Palais Royal,* a sort of guide to " that high 'Change of the fashion-able dissipation and vice of Paris," and perhaps characterized too severely by a contemporary critic as "a book with the particulars of which he would not sully his pen."   Also in 1819, we have the *Humourist, a Collection of Entertaining Tales, &c.,* in four volumes, now almost unfindable, and prized alike for the mellow humour of the coloured plates, and the racy wit of the well-selected stories.

In 1824, George illustrated for Robins the *Tales of Irish Life.* From this, Thackeray reproduced two of the plates,—an " Irish Wake," and an " Irish Jig,"—and expressing some doubt as to whether " Mr. Cruikshank had had any such good luck as to see the Irish in Ireland itself," asserts that " he certainly had obtained a knowledge of their looks, as if the country had all his life been familiar to him ; " and referring to the former of the two plates, that " there is not a broken nose in the room that is not thoroughly Irish."

In the next year, he partly illustrated for Fairburn *The Universal Songster or Museum of Mirth*, probably the most extensive collection of songs in the language ; and in 1825-7, the two series of *Mornings in Bow Street*. These volumes consist of a selection of the more humourous of the Bow Street Police Reports, which had been during the past three years contributed to the *Morning Herald* by Mr. J. Wight, reporter to that journal ; just as a subsequent reporter to the same paper, the late George Hodder, in 1845, made up an amusing volume *(Sketches of Life and Character taken at Bow Street Police Court,)* in a similar manner, with the illustrations of Leech, Kenny Meadows, Hamerton, Henning, and others. To these volumes Cruikshank contributed forty-six designs, all cut on wood by Thompson, Branston, Hughes and White, excepting the frontispiece to each volume, which was etched on copper by the artist. For the larger designs, the artist received five guineas each ; for the smaller, two guineas ; and, *more suo*, he has given his own portrait on the title-page vignette of Vol. I. The cuts are in George's best style, the stories well selected and well-told. I hardly, indeed, know a better " cordial for low spirits " than these humourous volumes ; or believe, that with them before him, Heraclitus himself could long remain 'αγέλαστος. There is a re-issue in 1875, with a preliminary essay by Mr. G. A. Sala.

In 1826, appeared *Greenwich Hospital: a Series of Naval Sketches illustrative of the Life of a Man of War's Man. By an Old Sailor.* (Captain Barker.) with a dozen capital etchings. Cruikshank, who dearly loved to poke fun at the soldiery, had a sort of family love for sailors and nautical life. His mother, as I have said before, was a sailor's daughter, and his brother Robert had passed a year or two at sea. George's earliest attempts at art were drawings. of ships ; and in the book I have mentioned, in *Tough Yarns* by the same author, in the *Sailor's Progress*, in the *Sea-ballads* of the Dibdins, in Captain Glascock's *Land Sharks and Sea Gulls*, in Captain Chamier's *Ben Brace*, in Mary Cowden Clarke's *Kit Bam's Adventures, or the Yarns of an Old Mariner*, and *The Old Sailor's Jolly-Boat*, he has depicted life at sea with amazing force and loving accuracy ; here, as in his transcripts from land-life, storeing up records of men, things, costume and manners, which

ILLUSTRATIONS

OF

TIME.

BY

GEORGE CRUIKSHANK.

"THERE IS A TIME FOR ALL THINGS."

TEMPUS EDAX RERUM.

LONDON.

Published May 1st 1827 by the Artist 22 Myddelton Terrace Pentonville. Sold by Js Robins & Co Ivy Lane Paternoster Row.

will remain and increase in historic value, as their prototypes disappear from the scene, and become things of the past. Thackeray points to "the noble head of Nelson" in the *Family Library*, as a proof that the designer must have felt and loved what he drew ; and here I am reminded of the statement that a head of the hero, at the head of a broadside with his life, "acknowledged to be the most faithful of all the resemblances that have issued from the press," was "a compilation from busts, pictures and casual observation, (for he never sat to its author) by Cruikshank, the father of George of that name, the first of living caricaturists."*

A handsome folio volume has been much hawked about at various epochs, entitled *Cruikshankiana, being a Collection of the most celebrated Works of George Cruikshank.* This consists of upwards of eighty large etchings, of which the greater part are by George, and the remainder by his brother Robert, and by Richard Dighton. Here we have a series of social and political caricatures, much in the manner of Gillray, but inferior to him, including a set of eight curious plates entitled "Monstrosities," which exhibit the fashions between 1816 and 1827. These shew us the human form more hideously distorted than the wildest imaginings of old Bulwer, —(the physician, not the peer)—in his *Anthropometamorphosis* ; presenting the male and female dandies of the day in all the glory of swallow-tails and coal-scuttles, Brummellian cravats, Cossack trousers, Hessian boots, sandalled shoes, flower-pot hats, gigot sleeves, and Oldenburg bonnets. All this gives the book, even in its degradation, a permanent interest ; but to the collector it is well-nigh valueless, the plates having been worn-out and re-cut, and the original dates altered to 1835, the period of their reissue, by the then proprietor, Thomas McLean, of the Haymarket.

The year 1826 is memorable as marking the artist's "first appearance in the character of an author." This, according to Hone, who, in the *Every Day Book*, (vol II., page 1121), gives a genial review of his friend's admirable series of etchings, *The Illustrations of Phrenology.* In the following year he gave us the companion series, *Illustrations of Time.* In each of these we get between thirty and forty designs upon six plates, besides the engraved titles,

* *Somerset House Gazette*, by W. H. Pyne, vol. ii. p. 205.

and one and the other are now of such rarity and value, that a set of the former, published originally at some three half-crowns, fetched five guineas the other day at a sale at Sotheby's. In these plates the humour of the artist seems to have reached its culminating point; the etching is broad, simple, and effective; and the drawing admirable. Several of the designs were piratically appropriated by the editor of *Bell's Life in London*, (for which paper, by the way, Cruikshank never made a single drawing), and rudely copied in wood, helped to give currency to the once famous *Gallery of Comicalities*. The artist remonstrated, but got no redress.*

In 1828, Mr. Charles Wilson, who has given us the best discriminative Catalogue of Rembrandt's etchings, printed, for private circulation among his friends, a list of the engravings in his collection. For this, Cruikshank produced five admirable etchings. They are in his happiest manner, and represent, with the nicest apprehension and sympathy, various phases of the life of a collector. First we have the "Battle of Engravers;" then "Connoisseurs at a Print Shop," "Connoisseurs at a Print Stall," "Connoisseurs at a Print Sale;" and lastly, a representation of the "Old Print Room at the British Museum."

We have seen that this period may be held to indicate the commencement of the artist's career as an independent worker; and tracing his progress a few years farther on,—say to 1835, when the *Comic Almanack* made its first appearance, we find him in the full swing and maturity of his powers, producing in the following decade some of his most important art-work, whether we have regard to its quantity or quality. To the *Almanack* of 1839, Thackeray contributed his capital story, *Stubbs's Calendar; or, the Fatal Boots*, admirably illustrated by the etchings of Cruikshank, month by month through the year. The *Almanack* continued to make its annual appearance in its original and best form, a repertory of fun and humour, and containing some of the artist's best

---

* The *Phrenological Illustrations* were "republished for the artist" by F. Arnold, in 1843 the *Illustrations of Time* in the following year. The artist in his humorous little preface, states that he found the plates of these etchings—"first published nearly fifty years back —as well as those of *My Sketch Book, Mr. Lambkin, Scraps and Sketches*, &c. which he also reissued at the same period, "in excellent condition." He adds with regard to the *Phrenological Illustrations*, that, notwithstanding the attacks which had been made upon the science, "the organs represented would still hold their place," and that his own "organ of covetiveness" had had some influence in the republication.

work, till 1848, when it was issued in diminished size and at cheaper rate, under the editorship of Horace Mayhew. In 1850 another change took place; the price was raised to the original half-crown, the paper cover was replaced by ugly cloth, a coloured folding frontispiece was added, the number of etchings reduced, and the name of Henry Mayhew appeared upon the title-page. The issue of 1853 was edited by Robert B. Brough; and this closed the series. Every change of form, as I have noticed to be invariably the case in serials, was for the worse; and the public had evidently grown tired of the once popular favourite.

The year 1836 is memorable as marking an era in light literature by the appearance of the *Sketches by Boz;* and here begins the association between the greatest humouristic writer and artist the century has produced, which subsisting in the *Life of Grimaldi,* the *Pic-Nic Papers,* and *Oliver Twist,* we may regret was not more permanent and continuous. The first number of *Bentley's Miscellany* appeared in Jan., 1837, with Cruikshank's well-known design upon the wrapper. Maginn indited the "Song of the Cover," which heralded the achievements of *pen* and *pencil,* not those of the *gun :*—

> "Bentley, Boz, and Cruikshank stand,
>   Like expectant reelers;
> 'Music!' 'Play up!' pipe in hand,
>   Beside the *fluted* pillars!
> Boz and Cruikshank want to dance,—
>   None for frolic riper;
> But Bentley makes the first advance,
>   Because he pays the piper."
>   *The Bentley Ballads, p. 96.*

George illustrated in all fourteen volumes of this serial, contributing no less than one hundred and twenty-nine plates. These were to illustrate successively *Oliver Twist, Jack Sheppard, Guy Fawkes, The Ingoldsby Legends, Nights at Sea, Stanley Thorn,* and various miscellaneous articles. *Oliver Twist* made his first appearance in the second number of the *Miscellany,* February, 1837. In these celebrated designs, which are too well known to need individualization, the artist may be said to have shown an inventive capacity equal to that of the writer. He has here manifested his supreme competence to depict the low, squalid, criminal, and tragic aspects of that life he knew so well,—his instinctive seizure upon the most dramatic incidents,—and his power of suggesting a complete story by a few isolated and striking scenes. Here, it may be observed, it is Dickens who is the caricaturist, not Cruikshank. It is only in accordance with the Horatian precept* that whatever obtains access to the mind through the eyes produces a more vivid impression than that which reaches it through the ears; and thus we are apt to be struck by exaggeration in design when we ignore a far larger amount of the same characteristic in literature. Cruikshank's illustrations, I contend, are literal transcripts of actual life; while the writings of Dickens, with all their pleasure-giving, improving, humanizing qualities, are full of the grossest exaggeration and caricature.

Of the admirable designs to illustrate *Oliver Twist* none is better known or more admired than that which represents " Fagin in the Condemned Cell." The wish may possibly be felt that the author had transferred to his narrative some of the " terrible distinctness " with which the "points" against the unhappy old man were urged in court, so that the crime for which he was to suffer might be more clearly seen; but with regard to the artist, it is generally admitted that he has managed to inform this little work, of a few square inches of size only, with such an amount of character, suggestiveness, and expression as to constitute it one of his master-pieces,

" —————— The dreadful Jew
That Cruikshank drew, —

gnawing his finger-ends like a caged rat, in the impotence of despair, haunted by the memories of an evil life, and sore beset by the agony of baffled revenge. The idea has somehow got abroad that here again the artist has perpetuated his own lineaments, when transferring to copper his idea of this most vicious and miserable character. The improbable story, in which there is but a shadow of truth, doubtless arose in the following wise. The prototype of Fagin was a blear-eyed, rusty-looking old Jew,—one of the red-haired type—whom the "great George" had often noted in the

---

* " Segnius irritant animos demissa per aurem,
Quam quæ sunt oculis subjecta fidelibus ————
HORAT. *De Arte Poeticâ.*

neighbourhood of Saffron-Hill.   To make this sordid character express by the natural language of attitude and occupation the emotions appropriate to that supreme hour of suffering, proved a task of unusual difficulty to the artist.   He laboured at the subject for several days without success, and almost thought of giving it up in despair.   It happened, however, that one morning, as he sat up in bed, stroking his chin with his hand, and nibbling his finger nails, the very image of puzzled dubitation, all at once he caught sight of the reflection of his face in a glass, and saw that chance offered him the very thing he had looked for in vain.   Leaping from his bed with all the exultation of Archimedes from the bath, he proceeded to fix the idea upon paper ; and to this fortuitous accident, as he himself related to Horace Mayhew, we are indebted for one of his most felicitous and remarkable designs.*

Here I may take occasion to notice that terrible piece of graphic realism,—sketched, we are told, upon the spot—" The Knacker's Yard, or the Horse's last Home," which is pronounced by a competent authority " scarcely below Rembrandt in force and largeness of style, while it is informed by an earnestness of purpose which the art of Rembrandt never aims at,"—the critic adding that " in this respect, Cruikshank has a close affinity to Bewick."†   This admirable plate, marred somewhat in effect by the weak drawing of the most prominent horse, appeared originally in Vol. III. of the *Voice of Humanity* (1831), and was thence transferred to the well-intentioned *Elysium of Animals* (1836) of the late Egerton Smith, of Liverpool.   Of this etching I have the pleasure of presenting to my readers a most excellent facsimile, which, though executed upon wood, exhibits in a marked degree, the force, the expression, and the character of the original.

I must dismiss with a bare mention the *Life of Grimaldi*, the *Minor Morals* of Dr. Bowring, and that delicious little tome, the *Sunday in London*, (1833) written by George's "dear friend," Mr. Wight, of the *Morning Herald*.   This book is very rare, the wood blocks and remaining stock having been destroyed by a fire at the publisher's, Effingham Wilson, of the Strand.

---

*Memories of My Time. By George Hodder, 1870, page 108.
† *Essays in Art*, by F. T. Palgrave, p. 181.

With like brevity must be dismissed the most admirable *Scraps and Sketches,* and *My Sketch Book,* with the remarkable etching of the "Gin Juggernaut," significant, with "The Fiend's Frying Pan,"* "The Gin Trap," and many others, of the artist's growing abhorrence of that vice, antagonism to which was to claim and absorb the vigour of his later years.

In 1838, he supplied eight illustrations to an enlarged edition of "Delta" Moir's exquisite piece of Scotch humour, the *Life of Mansie Wauch, Tailor in Dalkeith.* Here I may adopt a sentence from the preface—"Of the illustrations what shall we say? Nothing. They speak for themselves."

Meantime a quarrel, I know not from what cause, had taken place between Cruikshank, and Richard Bentley, the publisher; and by and by the artist thought that he had good cause of complaint also against W. Harrison Ainsworth, the well-known novelist. The latter had written his romance, *Old St. Paul's,* for the *Sunday Times;* the proprietors of which had engaged to pay him a sum of £1000 for his work. Now this very subject, George asserts, had been suggested by him to his literary associate, and the book was to have been published conjointly by them as partners. By and by, the copyright reverting to the author, the novel was issued in separate form, in the orthodox three octavo volumes. Of course George was out of the question as illustrator; so the able pencil of Mr. J. Franklin was secured. Thus George had the mortification,—to use his own words—of seeing "another artist working out his pet subjects, which he had nursed in his brain for many years, and which he had long intended to have placed before the public with his own hands." *Hinc illæ lacrymæ;* George determined to close with Ainsworth for good, and see what he could do on his own account. This was the origin of his monthly shilling serial *The Omnibus,* which he began to run in 1841, with poor

---

* This clever etching was one of the successful attempts which the artist took to himself credit for making with the object of "improving the customs of society." Taking "a peep on one or two occasions" at Bartholomew Fair, formerly held in Smithfield market annually, he was so disgusted at the "wild drunken blackguard ruffianism—too gross and too bad to be described," which prevailed there, that he produced this design, and dedicated it to the Lord Mayor and Aldermen of London, by long usage its patrons. By and by the Fair was abolished; and that of similar character, held at Greenwich, shortly afterwards suffered the same fate.

Pit Boxes & Gallery.

Designed, Etched. & Published by George Cruikshank
23 Myddelton Terrace Pentonville

not a page yet from the Printer
and I am more behind than ever

My dear Blanchard June 18th/44.
As I have been in hourly
expectation of seeing you, I did
not forward the enclosed to you:
which you will see requires an
immediate answer — I have
written to the author. Att[?] him
that he may depend upon having
an answer this day - certainly not
later than tomorrow morng. — shall
I see you to day..? Yours truly
Geo Cruikshank

Laman Blanchard—another fine genius ruined !—as conductor, at a salary of twenty guineas a month. The first number gave a highly idealized portrait of the artist, with an amusing paper, which, if inspired, was certainly not written by him, commenting with much humour upon certain silly gossip about his appearance and habits in which a contemporary had indulged. The *Omnibus* only reached one volume, the last number of which contained the admirable Rembrandtesque plate, the "Jack O'Lantern,"—a "gem of jet," as poor Walter Thornbury calls it,—"in which was focussed more genius than many a May Exhibition could claim in all its pictures." At this point a reconciliation was effected between the artist and his *quondam* associate, by the good offices of the late Thomas James Pettigrew, surgeon, and librarian to the Duke of Sussex. Ainsworth was anxious to start a "monthly" of his own ; and persuaded George to join him, and "drive his *Omnibus,* into the new magazine." This appeared in 1842 ; and if by his former conduct the editor had afforded the artist just cause of complaint, he certainly made honourable amends in his "preliminary address." In allusion to the latter he says :—

"In securing the co-operation of this admirable artist, the strongest assurance is given, not only of unequalled excellence in tragic and humourous illustrations, but of an anxious and thoughtful responsibilty in the exercise of that power. No work can need a surer guarantee than that which is conveyed in the association of an artist, who has passed an important period of his life in satirizing and ridiculing human follies, without giving one moment's pain to a fellow-creature ; who has faithfully delineated almost every diversity of character, without creating a single enemy. GEORGE CRUIKSHANK will be the illustrator of AINSWORTH'S MAGAZINE."

Notwithstanding this new alliance, and the disagreement existing between the artist and Mr. Bentley, the contract as to the production of a certain number of designs for the old "Miscellany" still remained in force. But these became very poor, the artist adhering to the letter, rather than the spirit of his undertaking ; and they are, perhaps, not unfairly characterised by the witty and learned "Father Prout" (Rev. Francis Mahony) as

"The designs so poor and scratchy
Of the Cruikshanks, his Caracci."

in some verses, which Mr. Sala enables me to quote, satirising, on behalf of the new Burlington Street serial, Ainsworth, Cruikshank, and the rival magazine.

The first novel that appeared in " Ainsworth " was the *Miser's Daughter*, exclusively illustrated by George, who contributed to it twenty etchings. The next, *Windsor Castle*, also contains designs by him ; but this had been commenced during the author's estrangement from the artist. Hence etchings for the earlier numbers had been commissioned in Paris from Tony Johannot, a very admirable French designer, well known for his excellent illustrations to Cervantes, Molière, and a host of foreign classical works ; vignettes on wood were also contributed by a graceful draughtsman, the late William Alfred Delamotte, drawing-master at the Military College, Sandhurst. Then came *St. James's, or the Court of Queen Anne*, which was the last romance which George illustrated for Ainsworth, as the latter thereupon sold the magazine to his publishers, to the infinite chagrin of the artist, and in violation, as he would imply, of a tacit understanding between them. Be this as it may, George illustrated altogether seven novels for Ainsworth,—including a re-issue of *Rookwood*, the original edition of which was published before the commencement of his acquaintance with the novelist. These, in chronological order, are :—(1) *Rookwood*. (2.) *Jack Sheppard*. (3) *Guy Fawkes*. 4.) *The Tower of London*. (5) *The Miser's Daughter*. (6) *Windsor Castle*. (7) *St. James's, or the Court of Queen Anne;* and for them he had made—to use his own words—" ONE HUNDRED AND FORTY-FOUR of the very best designs and etchings which he had ever produced." When he suspended the monthly issue of the *Omnibus*, he promised that it should appear as an annual volume ; but it was now suggested by his publishers (Messrs. Bradbury and Evans) that " as it was such a long time since the *Omnibus* had been on the road, it would, perhaps, be better to start another vehicle of the *same build*, but under another name." " To this I agreed," says he, " and thus originated *The Table Book*, which was edited by my friends, the late Gilbert A'Beckett and Mark Lemon."

The etched illustrations in this handsome volume, which bears date 1845, are very admirable, barring a growing puerility of sentiment. The one entitled "Sic Transit" is, however, in the artist's best style, free, vigorous, and natural; and the first in the book, "The Triumph of Cupid," gives an excellent portrait of the artist seated in "a reverie" before his fire-place, and smoking a huge pipe, in the fumes from which are developed hundreds of tiny figures, in various conditions of subjection to the mighty son of Venus. This was in George's unregenerate days, while yet a lover of the weed, for he says in his opening paper that "if his brain is ever illuminated by an electric spark, the bowl of his meerschaum is the place in which it is deposited; the pipe acting as a conductor, along which flashes- of inspiration are conveyed with every whiff, while the smoke curls itself into a variety of objects." This etching is also remarkable for the executive elaboration of its detail—though in this respect, like that other curiosity of etching, "Passing Events, or the Tail of the Comet of 1853," and certain plates of this period and later, finish and minuteness are perhaps carried further than the style of the artist could bear without deterioration. Another most admirable plate demands something more than a passing notice, before I put the *Table Book* out of my hands. This is inscribed the "Folly of Crime," and represents, as the centre-piece, a murderer, knife in hand, falling into an abyss in pursuit of a bowl of treasure, held aloft by a mocking demon, eluding, by his own descent, the frenzied grasp of the madman. Winged fiends exultingly hover above; and in compartments around, the rewards of crime are strikingly depicted. Of this piece an able critic remarks :—" There seems to me quite as much thought, and heart, and moral power about this work, as about any of Hogarth's or Dürer's; and I am firmly convinced that Cruikshank, when he dies (which may God long avert), and death has given a sacred character to his works, in our national collection of English art (if we ever have one) will be one of our most venerated old masters." *

A new edition of both *The Omnibus* and *The Table Book* was issued in 1869, by Messrs. Bell and Daldy.

The same year marks the appearance of Maxwell's graphic *History of the Irish Rebellion* in 1798, with twenty most admirable

---

* *British Artists from Hogarth to Turner.* By Walter Thornbury. Vol. II. p. 64.

illustrative etchings.   The original drawings for these, finished works
of art of marvellous delicacy and feeling, are now preserved in the
Westminster Aquarium.   As for the etchings, I do not know that
the artist has ever produced anything more remarkable, whether
we regard the technical excellence of the work, the marvellous
comprehension of Irish character, or the dramatic intensity of the
awful scenes depicted.   I have seen it recorded as a saying of Sir
Edwin Landseer, that John Leech never produced a drawing
unworthy of the honour of a frame ; surely with yet greater truth
the same may be asserted of the designs of George Cruikshank.

In 1848, Cruikshank, who had already embraced the Temperance
cause, though I hardly think that he had finally cast in his lot with
the total abstainers, produced his celebrated *Bottle*, with, shortly
after, its sequel *The Drunkard's Children*.   Here, in sixteen plates,
with a poetical commentary by Dr. Charles Mackay, is traced the
progress of a Drunkard and his family, from comfort and respecta-
bility to the Beerhouse, the Pawn-shop, the Asylum, the Court,
the Hulks and the River.   With much of Hogarth's narrative
talent, no small dramatic power, and the artist's own skill in composition and the exhibition of character, the series is yet somewhat
unsatisfactory, whether as a work of art, or as a moral lesson.   The
expected largeness of demand precluded the use of the copper-plate ;
and wood, which should have been the material used, was held,
I suppose, too costly.   Thus recourse was had to "glyphography," a
process by which engraved lines lose their definition, distance its
gradation, and the whole effect is rendered flat and lifeless.
Hence the procedure, with which, moreover, the artist at the time
was unacquainted, has now been practically abandoned.   Moreover as works of art the designs have a certain coarseness and
vulgarity, much of which is inevitable ; there is too much
sensationalism throughout ; and the eventuation, as Mr. Sala has
ably shewn, is melodramatic rather than tragic.   Dickens himself,
has recorded his opinion that " the philosophy of the thing as a
great lesson is all wrong."

The *Bottle*, however, was a huge success ; sold in immense
numbers (100,000 are said to have been disposed of in a day or two,
at a shilling each) ; was dramatized and represented at eight London

THE DRUNKARD'S CHILDREN.

PLATE II. —— BETWEEN THE FINE FLARING GIN PALACE AND THE LOW DIRTY BEER SHOP, THE BOY THIEF SQUANDERS AND GAMBLES AWAY HIS ILL-GOTTEN GAINS.

theatres simultaneously. The artist no doubt made hay during the brief sunshine ; though on exporting a large edition to America, he found that a pirated issue had already taken possession of the market.

In witnessing the representation of this piece upon the stage, one was once more struck with the artist's special talent for seizing upon the most dramatic situations of the story for the exercise of the pencil. Moncrieff,—so the tale goes*—when he dramatized " Tom and Jerry " for the Adelphi, wrote his piece from Cruikshank's plates, and " boiled his kettle with Egan's letter-press ; " and half a century later, Andrew Halliday, adapting *The Miser's Daughter* of Ainsworth for the same theatre, made up his most effective scenes from the designs of the artist. It was on witnessing the performance of this latter, and finding that his part in its production was totally ignored, that George was incited to make that public vindication of his claim to a share in the authorship of this and other works— notably *Oliver Twist*— illustrated by him, which, involving the candour and justness of Dickens, Ainsworth and himself, forms a noteworthy and characteristic episode in the latter part of his artistic career. Of this I shall have something to say further on.

Right or wrong in the teaching, a vast influence for ultimate good must have been exercised by this celebrated series, *The Bottle* and its sequel. Society, in its daily indulgence, was pervaded by a shock like that from the stroke of a gymnotus. The plates, in spite of their poverty of execution, were in the hands of every one, —the Theatre was crowded nightly by the *profanum vulgus*,— while the more critical scholar in his library was equally moved by the homely pathos of the story :—witness Matthew Arnold's fine sonnet, " On seeing Cruikshank's picture of the Bottle."

A temperate man is apt to become intemperate when he attacks intemperance. George Cruikshank gave himself up, heart and soul, to the cause ; and was ready with gratuitous help,—or what amounted to this—to any one that sought it. A volume would be needed to chronicle his labours in the cause of Temperance. Thus he volunteered to illustrate a series of letters on the *Domestic Habits of the People* (C. Gilpin, 1852.) published at a shilling,

* *Every Night Book ; or Life after Dark*, 1827. (" Cribb's Crib," p. 81.)

and produced for the purpose six full page designs, fairly cut on wood. He illustrated in like manner the well-known sixpenny pamphlet of Mr. J. W. Kirton, of Birmingham, *How Sam Adams's Pipe became a Pig,* which concludes with the advice that " smoked bacon is much more profitable than smoked pipes, whether they be *mere* shams or real *shams,*"—that " chewing *pig-tail* should be given up, and *real returns* sought for,"—and so the profit realized of changing a " *Pipe into a Pig !*"

As another of the artist's " counterblasts " may be mentioned a clever etched sheet, measuring about 11in. by 8in., and published without date, by Bogue, of Fleet Street. This is inscribed " Tobacco Leaves, No. 1," and is surmounted by a row of heads, over which is the legend, " Men and Gents (who are really respectable) may now be seen smoking in the streets, even with blackguard short clay pipes,—a practice which was formerly only indulged in by Sweeps and Dustmen ! Put that in your pipe and smoke it." At the foot is a group of school-lads, bowl in hand, and satchel on back, all smoking ; these are entitled " Early Pipers." The rest of the sheet is filled up with groups exhibiting in various ways the ridiculous and offensive aspects of the growing habit.

An " Illustrated Penny Reading," *The Gin Shop* (Partridge & Co.) is worthy of special note. Half a century ago George had illustrated *The House that Jack Built,* a satire on political mis-doing ; and now we have a like formula utilized in castigation of a social vice :—

" This is the *Gin-Shop* all glittering and gay,"

is the subject of a capital full page wood-cut ; then another shows us

"* * * The Drinks that are sold night and day,
At the bar of the Gin-shop, so glittering and gay."

next

"* * * the *Customers,* youthful and old, &c."

then

"* * * the *Landlord* that wins his bright gold
Out of the ruin of youthful and old, &c."

and

"* * * the *Lady,* all jewels and lace,
The wife of the Landlord who coins his bright gold, &c."

now comes

"* * * the *Drunkard,* in rags and disgrace," &c.

and
next

       " *   *   *   the *Woman* with wobegone face, &c.

       " *   *   *   the *Pastor*, so noble and kind, &c."

who brings with him

       " *   *   *   the *Paper* the poor drunkard signed," &c.

while the twelfth plate shows us, as the result of signing the pledge :—

       " *   *   *   the *Cottage*, the home of delight

         Whence prayer, like an incense ascends day and night, &c."

—altogether not a bad penny-worth, as " Cruikshanks " go !

Among the more distinguished supporters of the Temperance cause are two well-known writers who have shed over their advocacy the charm of culture and refinement, and whose literary efforts, during an united career of over half a century, have ever been in the interests of civilization and humanity. I allude to Mr. and Mrs. S. C. Hall. When Mr. Hall, a few years ago, published his *Trial of Sir Jasper, a Temperance Tale in Verse,* some three and twenty of the first artists of the day made special designs in illustration and aid. Among these are the names of E. M. Ward and his wife, Elmore, Faed, Dobson, Noel Paton, Gilbert, Tenniel, Birket Foster, Gustave Doré, Cave Thomas and others. Among these, George Cruikshank, whose friendship with the author extended over a period of nearly sixty years, contributed a most characteristic design, admirably cut in wood by the brothers Dalziel, to illustrate the lines, descriptive of the condition of the drunkard-scholar :—

      " Ten thousand devils haunt him, day and night,

        Haunt him alike in darkness and in light."

In like manner, when Mrs. Hall, in 1875, collected some of the most effective of her long published Temperance stories, the name of George Cruikshank is again found among the fifteen distinguished artists who collaborated to illustrate a like number of tales.

At the epoch of the publication of *The Bottle*—to retrace my steps from the anticipatory advance I have been tempted to make—the artist was approaching the conclusion of his sixth decade ; the season of creative productiveness was drawing to a close ; and thenceforth, with no diminished capacity for work, he seemed rather to seek a motive impulse from the ideas of others, or devoted himself to the advocacy of that noble cause to the furtherance of which his energies were gradually narrowing.

Before, however, proceeding to the next division of my subject, I must not omit to mention his magnificent etching of the " Opening of the Great Exhibition," on May 1, 1851. The view is taken from the South West Gallery, and the time chosen is that in which the Archbishop offers up a prayer for the Divine Blessing on the objects of the undertaking. The plate measures 16-in. by 10-in., and is remarkable for its vast multiplicity of detail, and the immense number and variety of figures which the artist has crowded together without confusion. The same event also suggested Harry Mayhew's volume, *The World's Show, 1851, or the Adventures of Mr. and Mrs. Sandboys and Family.* This was published monthly, and extended to ten parts, each containing a large folding etching, the first of which, " All the World going to see the Exhibition," is a marvel of microscopic elaboration and minuteness.

I cannot pretend to enter at length into the much-vexed, but really unimportant question of George Cruikshank's claim to have been the " originator " of the *Oliver Twist* of Charles Dickens, and the *Miser's Daughter* and other of the romances of W. Harrison Ainsworth. The assertion of this claim, with its contemptuous treatment by Mr. Forster, and the " positive and flat contradiction " of Mr. Ainsworth, placed the artist, as he tells us, " in a very serious position as regards his character for truthfulness and the condition of his intellect ;" and he felt compelled, in self defence, to issue in 1872 his pamphlet, *The Artist and the Author, a Statement of Facts* (Bell and Daldy). Here he positively asserts that, in the novels I have mentioned and others, he was the actual "originator of the ideas and characters," and that the authors " wrote up to his suggestions and designs "—just, in fact, as Combe, in *Dr. Syntax,* is known to have done with regard to the previously executed illustrations of Rowlandson.

To what extent this may have been the case, it is now impossible to determine. That George Cruikshank was an entirely truthful and honourable man, no one that knew him will deny ; and that, tenacious as he undoubtedly was with regard to his own rights and the recognition due to his talents, it was utterly impossible that, knowingly, he could put forward a claim to that which was not his own. Any way, there can be no reasonable doubt that, in the frequent intercommunication between the men, the ideas and designs of each would undergo influence and modification ; and that those of the artist, as the older and more experienced, would often prevail. But the extent to which this took place is surely a matter of little moment ; and the latter might well take consolation, as I once endeavoured to convince him, by turning to the columns of any bookseller's catalogue, where, under *his* name, as that which gave the books their currency and value, the various authors he has illustrated are all ranked. This is true also in the case of the *magna nomina* of Dickens and Ainsworth ; with whom most assuredly will George Cruikshank

> "Pursue the triumph and partake the gale,"

as "artist and author," in indissoluble connection, sail together down the "stream of fame."

(From an Original Pencil Drawing.)

VI.

Book Illustrations.—Under this head I include all designs which are not, like those of the *Sketches* and *Oliver Twist*, pictures of contemporary social life and character, but depend rather upon imagination and study than the artist's own faculty of observation. The earliest of these that I shall notice is also one of the best and most important. This is a volume, dear in each sense of the word to the collector, the *Points of Humour*, published in 1823 by C. Baldwyn, of Newgate Street—whose daughter, Eliza, became the artist's second wife and survives him. The "Points" were ten in number, each illustrated by a full-page etching, besides wood-cut vignettes or tail-pieces. In the following year appeared a second part, equal in extent to the former. If the "humour" is capital—we have the "Jolly Beggars" of Burns (rejected by the too fastidious Currie, and slipping through the meshes of Cromek's draw-net), with selections from Shakspeare, Fielding, and others—the illustrations are not less admirable. Some defective "biting" in the etchings may be here and there discernible; but they are broad and vigorous in touch, full of colour, and excellent in light and shade; while the smaller vignette *capricci* are worthy, in fantastic character and sprightliness of action, of the needle of Callot, or Della Bella. Looking at these excellent etchings, and others of the same kind, I am disposed to regard George Cruikshank as then at his best, and question whether he made any absolute advance after this early epoch. Mentally, as well as physically, man, as a rule, attains his maximum stature at the end of the second decade of his existence. Growth then ceases; and development, a slower and less obvious process, sets in. In literature, in fine art, in the handicrafts, if we assume any numeric symbol to indicate the extent of attainment possible to an individual, we shall find that he has well nigh reached it at five and twenty; and that his farther approaches thereto in after-life are slow and uncertain—if indeed he do not retrogress. Not but that there are late minds, which may appear exceptions to the rule; but even here we may in great measure predicate the future from the present, and feel sure that what is not great or good now never will be. Moreover in art—and it is to this that these remarks especially refer—what is gained is chiefly in the way of elaboration and executive skill, and this is balanced by a loss of spontaneity and creative energy. Thus I feel justified in expressing a preference for the artist's earlier style of work, with its vigour, freehandedness and simplicity, to the more laboured productions of a later day, where a greater technical skill is often shown at the expense of breadth, and finish not infrequently degenerates into mannerism and "spottiness."

In 1824 our artist produced the sixteen admirable wood-cut designs for the *Italian Tales of Humour, Gallantry, and Romance*, "illustrated," said the *Westminster Review* (No. I.), "with a grace which, without imitation, approaches the beauty of Stothard's compositions."* The same year gives us *Der Freischütz Travestie*. By Septimus Globus, (pseudonym for T. A. Apel,) with twelve etchings by George Cruikshank, from drawings by A. C., an Amateur ("Alfred Crowquill"). Both this, and the preceding work, were also published by C. Baldwyn, of Newgate Street.

In 1828 he executed twenty-four vigorously etched plates to illustrate the ancient drama of *Punch and Judy*, prefaced by a readably learned dissertation upon its origin, and that of puppet-plays in England, by the veteran literator, John Payne Collier. For the special benefit of author, artist, and publisher (Septimus Prowett, of Pall Mall,) a matutinal performance of the time-honoured comedy of Punchinello was got up by "an old Italian wayfaring puppet showman of the name of Piccini, who had perambulated town and country for the last forty or fifty years"; and whose manipulation of the familiar *dramatis personæ*—so George, who had known him from childhood, states—was far superior to anything of the kind to be seen at the present day. Like the pieces of our own early drama, the representation was not divided into acts and scenes. The proper divisions were made however by Mr. Collier, who took down the dialogue as the show proceeded; while the artist effected stoppage at the most telling parts to sketch the figures. The only account extant of Piccini is to be found in an old periodical called *The Literary Speculum*; Mr. Collier alludes briefly to him in his

---

* Facing page 58 should be found a wood-cut design inscribed "The Dead Rider." Here, within a tumble-down shed, may be dimly descried a dead monk enthroned on a *sedes stercoraria*, while another without, incensed at his delay, hurls a stone at him. It needs the context to tell us this much ; but the plate was withdrawn in the later issues.

"Preface"; and the artist has handed down his outward man to posterity in the vignette on the title-page—replaced, it may be noticed, in the 4th edition of *Punch and Judy* (Lacy, Strand) in consequence of the absence or loss of the original block, by a design from the pencil of his brother Robert. There is yet a 5th edition, with coloured plates, published in 1870 by Bell and Daldy; and a German translation, from the Stuttgart press, in 1865.

In 1828, also appeared *Eccentric Tales from the German of W. F. Von Kosewitz*, with twenty coloured etchings, worthy of special mention as being also the joint work of George Cruikshank, and the clever artist known by the pseudonym of "Alfred Crowquill"*

In 1830, we have *Tales of Other Days*; and the same year gave us a charming volume, of which Thackeray says that it contains "some of the best designs of our artist, and some of the most amusing tales in our language." This is the *Three Courses and a Dessert* of the late William Clarke, a writer who died very early, and to whose original and happy vein of humour due attention has not been given. The numerous illustrations to this volume, besides their excellence in design, are very triumphs of xylography. Here too, as elsewhere, may be noticed the artist's special faculty of imparting characteristic vitality to all sorts of odds and ends—a mug of ale, a wig-block, a pair of spectacles, a cut lemon, a bottle-cork, an oyster, and a mushroom—though I am not unaware that for the original ideas of some of these the author himself takes credit.

Mr. Clarke was also author of the *Cigar*, a genial little book, in which under the heading, "The Young Hogarth," a short article is devoted to the merits of the artist. "Some years ago," says he, "I was laughed at for predicting that George Cruikshank would, ere long, come into especial notice. George is a singular fellow; he is never conscious of his fine touches." In the *Boy's Own Book* by the same author,—the best book ever written for lads,—I fancy I recognize the hand of Cruikshank among the excellent designs; and to his *Every Night Book*, (1827)—one of the most genial, witty, and thoroughly typical opuscles of the day, conveying, as it seems to me, the very form and pressure of the time,—George

---

* The actual name of this gentleman was Alfred Henry Forrester. He died in May, 1872. in the 67th year of his age.

contributed the fantastic vignette on the title-page. In this racy volume we find another generous tribute by the author to his artist-friend. In his capacity of mystagogue to the nocturnal haunts of London, he conducts us to "Belcher's"—the Castle Tavern, Holborn—where most did congregate the fistic heroes of the day. Here we are introduced to Hickman the Gas man, Dutch Sam, Richmond the black, Peter Crawley, Jack Scroggins, Frosty-faced Fogo, white-headed Bob, Bill Eagles, and Jackson himself,— commander-in-chief! A well-known phiz appears amid the motley throng :—"'Ah, George, how are you?'—That person to whom we have just spoken, with nothing particular about him but his paleness, is our young Hogarth—George Cruikshanks, the matchless, delightful Cruikshanks.* Well! go thy ways, young blade, with our hearty benison upon thee. We have laughed, until laughter hath become a pain to us, at thy productions ; and in gratitude for the jocund moments thy pencil hath afforded us, we would, an' we could even take a wrinkle from thy brow and place it on our own." (Page 40.)

With the sympathetic intelligence which enabled him to grasp so perfectly the ideas of other minds, Cruikshank illustrated Fielding, Smollett, and Goldsmith, for the "Novelist's Library" of Thomas Roscoe, (1831-2, in 17 vols., 8vo.) These excellent etchings, forty-one in number, were issued by Tilt, the publisher, in 1832, in separate form, "for the benefit of collectors."

In 1836, appeared that capital tale, *The Adventures of Sir Frizzle Pumpkin*, by the Rev. Jas. White, with seven admirable etchings,— the one facing the title page presenting one of the best likenesses of the artist ; and in 1838, the *Gentleman in Black*, by the Rev. C. Clarke, of Esher, with its fine wood-cuts. Cruikshank, I may here take occasion to say, has been especially fortunate in the artists who have engraved his designs on wood. Among them are found the names of Williams, Landells, Branston, Thompson, Byfield, Wright, and Bonner ; and it is probably not too much to

---

*The father's name was often spelt "Cruickshanks," and the son had no little difficulty in getting rid of what he considered the superfluous letters. Christopher North in the "Noctes" (March, 1822) speaks eulogistically of "Little Cruikshanks "; here we have the author of the *Every Night Book*,—his own familiar friend,—talking of him in like manner ; and the reduplicated "c," on the title-page of the earlier copies of *Peter Schlemihl* will not fail to "fetch" your "coney-catching" collector !

say that it is beyond the power of art to effect more than these eminent xylographers have, in their day, achieved.

Differing altogether from his general style of work, and so worthy of especial notice, are the illustrations to *Burford Cottage,* (1835,) *Knickerbocker's History of New York*, and Defoe's *Journal of the Plague Year*, all now, if not originally, published by Tegg. The frontispiece to the first of these books, engraved on steel with much delicacy by Davenport, is so carefully drawn, and displays such refinement of humour, that it might be ascribed to Wilkie or Smirke ; and in *Knickerbocker*, George could hardly then have become a misocapnist when he limned with such intense *gusto* the " Pipe-Plot," with its group of smoke-compelling burghers, or the " Death of Walter the Doubter," where his lymphatic Excellency, lungs and pipe exhausted together, exhales his peaceful soul in the last whiff of canaster !

In 1840, appeared the once celebrated *Jack Sheppard* of W. H. Ainsworth. A century ago and more, the father-in-law of Hogarth went to Newgate to sketch, *ad vivum*, the youthful burglar. To borrow a quatrain from some doggrel of the day :—

> " Apelles, Alexander drew ;
> Cæsar, is to Arellius due ;
> Cromwell in Lely's work doth shine :
> And Sheppard, Thornhill, lives in thine ! "†

Of the series of etchings by which in our own day Cruikshank has given a new lease of immortality to the knight of the crowbar and centre-bit, so minute an analysis has been given by Thackeray in his *Westminster* paper,—the best essay on the artist yet written, and one on which we are told the writer looked back with peculiar satisfaction,—that any further notice is rendered nugatory. In this and the succeeding romances from the same hand some of the greatest triumphs of the artist's technical skill are supposed to be found. But I must confess that in many of the plates it seems to me that the machine-ruler has too completely elbowed out the etcher, and that finish has detracted from spontaneity and vigour while it has not added to fact. The same remarks may apply to the illustrations to *John Manesty*, a posthumous novel of the late William Maginn, originally published in *Ainsworth's Magazine*.

---

† *The Malefactor's Register, or New Newgate and Tyburn Chronicle, 8vo., page 108.*

In 1835-45, he illustrated the *Waverley Novels* (in 36 vols.,) for whlch he produced thirty-five spirited etchings.   These have been reproduced in several subsequent editions ; and may be obtained by the collector,—at least the greater part of them,—in the *Centenary Garland : Pictorial Illustrations of the Novels of Sir Walter Scott.*   (Edinburgh, Seton & Mackenzie, 1871.)—one of the numerous compilations suggested by the hundredth anniversary of the birth of the great novelist.

It is impossible to give more than the titles of a few among the innumerable books which Cruikshank has illustrated,—such as Defoe's *Robinson Crusoe,* Anstey's *Bath Guide,* Cowper's *John Gilpin, The Loving Ballad of Lord Bateman, The Bee and the Wasp,* Hood's *Epping Hunt,** Pettigrew's *Egyptian Mummies,* Reach's *Clement Lorimer,* Mayhew's *Whom to Marry, Tooth-Ache, The Magic of Kindness,* and *The Greatest Plague of Life,* Southey's *Life of Nelson,* Smith's *Rejected Addresses, The Bachelor's Own Book, or the Adventures of Mr. Lambkin,* Merle's *Odds and Ends, Tom Thumb, Bombastes Furioso, Hints on Etiquette, The Comic Alphabet, Works of Tim Bobbin,* a'Beckett's *Comic Blackstone,* Mrs. Gore's *Christmas Stories,* Smedley's *Frank Fairlegh,* Mrs. Stow's *Uncle Tom's Cabin,* Lowell's *Biglow Papers,* Raymond's *Life of Elliston,* Carlton Bruce's † *Mirth and Morality,* Auldjo's *Constantinople,* Douglas Jerrold's *Cakes and Ale,* Cholmondely Pennell's *Puck on*

---

* In Pierce Egan's *Book of Sports* (1832, 8vo) are some doggrel verses about Tom Rounding, " The Ever Green Sportsman of Woodford Wells," and Epping Hunt :—

> " All sorts of coves—fat, thin, and lank,
>   All in a merry mood :—
> Amongst them famed GEORGE CRUIKSHANK
>   And punning TOMMY HOOD.
> George with a pencil heav'd a sigh,
>   On sketching Tommy's frame—
> Said ' such a man should never die,
>   So great in hunting fame.' "   page 194.

† This is one of the " dull books about children," which Thackeray says " George Cruikshank makes bright with illustrations."   He cites the quatrain :—

> " Who has not chased the butterfly,
>   And crushed its slender legs and wings,
> And heaved a moralizing sigh ;
>   Alas ! how frail are human things ? "

and adds, " a very unexceptional morality truly ; but it would have puzzled another than George Cruikshank to make mirth out of it as he has done."   The book was planned at the table of Mr. Tegg, the publisher, where author and artist met.   " Carlton Bruce," " Peter Parley," and " Old Humphrey," were all alike pseudonyms of George Mogridge, a well known and most prolific writer for children.   He was born at Ashted, Birmingham, Feb. 17, 1787, and died Nov. 2, 1854.   Many of his books are published by the Religious Tract Society.

Pegasus, Daniel's *Modern Dunciad, Ferdinand Franck, Spirit of the Public Journals,* Lever's *Arthur O'Leary, The Cat's Tail, Beauties of Washington Irving,* Andrew Halliday's *Savage Club Papers,* Inglis's *Rambles in the Footsteps of Don Quixote,* O'Neill's *Drunkard, a Poem,* Friswell's *Out and About,* J. T. Akerman's *Tales of other Days, The Bentley Ballads, Remarks on Education* by Himself, *Fashion, Modern Belles,* Hoskyns's *Talpa, or Chronicles of a Clay Farm,* " cum multis aliis quæ nunc perscribere longum est."

In all these it may probably be said with truth that a comic element more or less exists ; but it is likely enough, as Maginn hints in *Fraser,* that Cruikshank,—like Liston and Charles Mathews (the elder), who thought their *forte* was Tragedy, —considered the Epic or Historic his proper domain. However this may be, I do not forget that Ruskin himself asserts that " his tragic power, though rarely developed and warped by habits of caricature, is, in reality, as great as his grotesque power." Thus, in a more serious branch of art, he has made designs for *Paradise Lost* and *Pilgrim's Progress** ; and I have before me a series of forty wood-cut designs, published by Robins in 1824, to illustrate George Clinton's *Life and Writings of Lord Byron.*

Here I am reminded of the fine series of plates, executed so recently as 1858, to illustrate Brough's *Life of Sir John Falstaff.* These are highly-laboured etchings, admirable alike in conception and execution. The first plate is one of the best of the set, and gives us the counterfeit presentment of the " whoreson fat man " himself; " Drawn by William Shakspeare and Etched by George Cruikshank ; " farther on we have the death-scene, where the " old white-bearded Satan " picks at the bed-clothes and babbles o' green fields as he nears his unhonoured end,—a masterpiece of sugges-

---

* Referring to one of the Milton illustrations—"Satan calling on the Fallen Angels"— Mr. J. Potter Briscoe, writing to *Notes and Queries* (5th S. IX. 434) transcribes a letter from the artist himself, in which the former speaks of this as " the best drawing he ever did in his life." The wood-block is missing ; but an impression from it is preserved (No. 16) in the Westminster Aquarium. I give the lines illustrated, which are ludicrously misquoted by Cruikshank himself in the Aquarium Catalogue :—

> " He call'd so loud that all the hollow deep
> Of Hell resounded * * * * * * * *
> ' Awake, arise, or be for ever fall'n !'
> They heard and were abash'd, and up they sprung
> Upon the wing, etc.

Paradise Lost, Book I. 314.

tiveness and pathos ; and lastly, the concluding plate, " Sir John Falstaff and the Fairies at Herne's Oak," one of the artist's most successful efforts in a walk of art in which he was truly *facile princeps,*—and of which, in due course, I come now to speak.

VII.

THE SUPERNATURAL.—Every man,—I mean a master and not a mere journeyman of nature—has his speciality. That is, there is some one thing,—only unfortunately he does not always know what it is, or knowing, has not an opportunity of doing it—which he can do better than any other man. In like manner, among the many things which a man has to do in his brief working day, there is some one thing which he can do better than anything else, and for which, of course, he seems especially fitted. This, as it appears to me, may be said of George Cruikshank as a delineator of the Supernatural. Not dealing with the *cognita et visa* which may be tested by the common perceptions of other observers, and a recognised standard of comparison, this is a branch of pictorial design which seems to escape many of the laws which govern generally the imitative arts. Here the draughtsman may give his inventive faculty play, indulge the wildest caprices of his imagination, and set the rules of anatomy, zoology and botany at defiance. Substance may exist without shadow, time and space be set at nought, and matter assume positions at utter variance with the Newtonian hypothesis. Surpassing the fantastic Callot, the dyspeptic Fuseli, the once fashionable Retzsch, and the unfortunate Dadd, George Cruikshank seems to me the best of all the artists who have made picturesque incursions into the regions of the Supernatural. Here again, in studying the genius of the man, we are struck above all with the wide range of its sympathies and capabilities. Whatever he undertook he appears to have entered into heart and soul ; so identifying himself with the characters, human or superhuman, which were the subject of his fantastic pencil, that landscape, buildings, accessories, appear to him as we may suppose they would to them, in their particular circumstances and conditions of being. Some such process of identification has to be gone through, consciously to unconsciously, by ourselves, before we can recognise the entire harmony, the perfect sense of fitness, which reigns throughout; and this apparently without the least effort or study. He seems to possess an intuitive knowledge—if I may so speak—of all that concerns Demonry, Fairydom and Wonderland; is as much at home in the realms of Oberon and Titania, as in Seven Dials or St. Giles's; and is just as conversant with the habits and doings of Witches, Fairies, Gnomes and Demons as those of the London Cockney or the Jew Fence. By royal sign-manual he was,—or deserved to be—sergeant-painter to Queen Mab herself, Puck, " Nimphidia and the Court of Fayrie." Landseer has been styled the Raphael of the canine race; and with equal justice may George Cruikshank be termed the Apelles of Hobgoblins, Pigwidgeons, Bull-beggars, Moon-calves, Sprites and Brownies,—the Zeuxis of Sylphs, Pixies, Kobolds, and the whole tribe of

> ————— ————— " Fairy Elves,
> Whose moonlight revels, by a forest side
> Or fountain, some belated peasant sees,
> Or dreams he sees, while over-head the Moon
> Sits arbitress, and nearer to the earth
> Wheels her pale course —— "
> —*Milton.*

So far back as 1824,[*] appeared Dr. Bowring's version of *Peter Schlemihl*, the story of a man who sold his shadow to the Devil. The reader of Pausanias[†] will recollect the olden belief that those daring wights who transgressed that part of Mount Lycæus which was sacred to Jupiter, lost the same ornamental appendage; so that a shadowless man was not a new idea. But the little book had the luck to appear just at a time when interest was awakened to German literature; it became very popular, and went through two or three editions. It appears to me somewhat overrated; and I should give preference to the quite recent *Case of Mr. Lucraft* of Walter Besant, where the appetite, instead of the shadow, is the object of sale. The appearance of the English edition, Dr. Bowring tells us, "thanks to the merit of Cruikshank's original and felicitous sketches," excited the greatest delight in the mind of Chamisso, the author; and in

---

[*] Collectors are anxious to secure *early* copies of the first edition, known by the printer's error in the name of the artist, where we find an adventitious "c"—" Cruickshank." The error was corrected after a few copies had been worked off.

[‡] Pausanias, *Arcadica.* lib. III. c. 38.

Pl 1

P. 20.

Designed Etched & published by George Cruikshank   Nov.r 1830.

The " Corps de Ballet "

Pl. 10

P. 312

Designed Etched & Published by George Cruikshank   Nov.r 1830

Witches Frolic

Designed Etched & Published by George Cruikshank Nov. 1830

"Tak aff the Ghaist!"

Designed Etched & Published by George Cruikshank Nov. 1830

Puck in Mischief —

1827 Hitzig writes to inform his friend Fouqué that "eine neue Ausgabe, mit den Zeichnungen der Englischen, die der berühmte CRUIKSHANK nach dem Leben entworfen, veranstaltet wird." This edition (Nürnberg, 1827, 8vo.,) is before me, with its six "kupfern," which are certainly marvels of reproductive assimilation.

In 1830 the appearance of Sir Walter Scott's *Letters on Demonology and Witchcraft* afforded the artist an opportunity of employing his imagination in a direction altogether congenial. Here he has given us a dozen etchings to accompany the volume, of the weirdest fancy and the most precious touch. It was a supper of raw pork, we are told, that begot upon the brain of Fuseli those gaunt and pallid forms that menacingly point or stride upon his neglected canvas in every attitude of agonistic horror; and our artist, one would think, had had recourse to a like expedient, for he seems himself a victim to *ephialtes* and to have embodied on copper the visions of his own disordered fantasy. Each plate tells its story so well that we little need Sir Walter's text for an explanation. Mr. Palgrave cites the "Witches' Voyage" (I suppose he means the "Frolic") as "a perfect masterpiece of humour, satire, and supernaturalism;" but my own favourites are the "Corps de Ballet," "Puck in Mischief," and "Tak aff the Ghaist!" Note, in the first, what frolicsome vitality is given to chairs and tables, and how the very walls seem reeling with adventitious life. Then, in the last, how absolutely complete is the artist's narration! The farmer, after his moonlight ride, has managed to reach the old Teviotdale homestead, the demented woman clinging like grim death to his girdle; the horse—who says G. C. cannot draw a horse?—is sore spent with his gallop and double burden; the gawky farm lads, sons maybe—the younger of course foremost—advance with the lantern; and the housewife at the door uplifts her hands in speechless horror. "Tak aff the Ghaist!" are the last words the poor man can utter ere he is carried off to his bed half dead with nervous shock. Mark the incurved tail of the jaded horse, and the twist in the foremost lad's leg to prevent propulsion by the elder looby. It is unconscious touches like these that denote true genius.

In 1823 appeared Edgar Taylor's selection from the *Kinder und Haus Mährchen* of the brothers Grimm, with twelve etchings; and three years later, a second series with ten more illustrations. Two or three editions were called for ; the etchings were reproduced in Germany ; and the first twelve copied in Paris by an ingenious Frenchman—a M. Ambrose Tardieu—who, in his admiration, forgot to mention that they were not the products of his own invention.* The two series were published at a dozen shillings, but are now so scarce and valued that clean copies are worth almost as many guineas. Perhaps of all the works of the master there is none so highly esteemed at home and abroad, or which extorts from the collector so fanciful a price. In 1868, the complete work was reissued, at the request of Mr. Ruskin, by the late J. C. Hotten, in tasteful form, and with the etchings so faithfully reproduced that, on actual inspection, they imposed on that renowned connoisseur ; and, as he himself told me, on the artist himself. Mr. Hamerton, in his *Etching and Etchers,* asserts that he "has not found their equal in comic etching any-where"; and Mr Ruskin, in the long introduction with which he has enriched Mr. Hotten's reprint, says they are " of quite excellent and sterling art—in a class precisely parallel in elevation to the character of the tales which they illustrate—unrivalled in masterful-ness of touch since Rembrandt—and in some qualities of delineation unrivalled even by him."

There is an admirable frontispiece, " Designed and Etched on Copper by George Cruikshank, and faced with steel by J. Goubert's acierage process," to Dr. Blakey's interesting volume, *Old Faces in New Masks,* (1859), in which may be seen two little groups, so grimly felicitous in their light and airy touch, that we may regret the artist did not give us a complete series to rival or even excel, the *Todtentanz* of Holbein, Machaber, and Rethel, the *Death's Doings* of Dagley, and the Death-Dance of Rowlandson and Van Assen.

I must pass with mere notice the wood-cuts for the *Fairy Tales* from the German of Albert Ludwig Grimm, (1827) the weird illus-trations to the English version of Victor Hugo's *Hans of Iceland,* (1825), those to the *Adventures of Münchausen,* the *True Legend of St. Dunstan,* the six exquisite etchings to J. E. Taylor's version

* The title of M. Tardieu's volume is *Vieux Contes pour l'amusement des Grands et des Petits Enfans, ornés de 12 Gravures Comiques.* Paris, A. Boulland, 1830.

of the *Pentamerone*, of Giambattista Basile, (a Neapolitan fairy-tale), (1848), Dudley Costello's *Holiday with Hobgoblins*, (1861), Keightley's *Fairy Mythology*, Hunt's *Popular Romances of the West of England*, *The Yule Log*, (a glyphographic failure), *The Brownie and other Tales*, and *Lob lie by the Fire*, by Juliana Horatia Ewing, and the *Discourse concerning Ghosts*, (1864) written, as well as illustrated, by the artist himself.

Moreover, scattered through many of the volumes noticed in other sections, will be found exquisite draughts of the Supernatural—in *Three Courses and a Dessert*, *Tom Thumb*, *Points of Humour*, *Tales of other Days*, *The Ingoldsby Legends*, and the Falstaff series to which I have already alluded. Philosophy and Science have tried hard to "pull the old woman out of our hearts," as Addison phrases it; nevertheless a love of, if not a belief in, Witches, Ogres, Giants, and Fairies, is still a survival among us. Thus Cruikshank's *Fairy Library*, ("Hop o' my Thumb," "Jack of the Bean Stalk," "Cinderella," and "Puss in Boots"), found other and graver admirers than "the little children," the "dear young ladies and gentlemen," whom the kindly artist, in his simple and affectionate address, said he had "through life done his best to amuse, and, if possible, instruct." The explanation which follows was extorted from him by a half-jocular paper in *Household Words*, entitled "Frauds on the Fairies," in which his old friend and ally, Charles Dickens, brought a charge against the artist of altering the hallowed text of these old stories to suit his own taste, and enable him to ventilate his peculiar crotchets. The defence of the artist was, that as Shakspeare and Scott had thought proper to alter Italian tales, and even history, to suit their purposes, he might surely take a like liberty with "a common Fairy-tale," especially with the object of removing unsuitable and objectionable passages, and inculcating moral principles. However this may be, the controversy occasioned a coolness between the friends which never wholly passed away; and the book is now valued for the exquisite illustrations alone. To enjoy these, however, in any degree, it is necessary to secure a fairly early copy; the book having been often republished, and, in later issues, the plates so worn, that scarcely any life or spirit remains in the impressions.

In 1853, George made an abortive attempt to establish a "Magazine" under his own name, with "Frank Fairlegh" (Mr. Frank E. Smedley) as editor. Only two numbers were issued ; but these are especially interesting, as containing, besides the etchings and wood-cuts, the artist's defence of his treatment of the "Fairy Tales," in reply to the paper of Dickens to which I have alluded.

VIII.

PAINTINGS IN OIL. Although it is not as an oil-painter that George Cruikshank will be known to posterity, any notice of him without some discussion of his capabilities and achievements in this direction would be incomplete. Always ambitious to attain distinction in the higher walks of art, for which he believed he had a special vocation, he would early have recourse to this noblest means of pictorial expression. All great artists have painted signs. Not to go back to Correggio, Holbein and Domenichino, Bonnell Thornton's exhibition, or the mythical Dick Tinto, Hogarth himself did not disdain to paint a sign for a "paviour," and "The Man loaded with Mischief" at 414, Oxford Street. Sam. Wale and Catton, both Royal Academicians, employed their brushes in a like manner ; as, in a later day, are said to have done, old Crome and David Cox. Ibbetson painted "The Tippler" at Troutbeck; Morland "The White Lion" at Paddington; Herring the same noble animal at Doncaster ; Wilson "The Three Logger-heads" at Mould ; Harlow "The Queen Charlotte" at Epsom ; Sir Charles Ross "The Magpie" at Sudbury ; and Millais "The Saint George and Dragon" at the little village of Hayes in Kent. So, in the storm and stress of the "Tom and Jerry" period, well-nigh sixty years ago, George thought it no shame to paint a full-length portrait of Walbourne, as "Dusty Bob," for a sign to his house, "The Maidenhead," Battle Bridge ; where, for aught I know, it may be swinging still. To the Royal Academy Exhibition of 1830, he contributed the subject "Fitting out Moses for the Fair"; in 1852, "Tam O'Shanter"; and in 1853, a scene from "Midsummer Night's Dream." He was also an occasional con-tributor to the British Institution. His picture, "Disturbing the

Congregation," purchased by, if not painted for, the Prince Consort, is well known from the engraving. Then there is a favourite piece, full of spirit and humour, "The Run away Knock"; and I remember a small picture (Grimaldi in a Barber's Shop, I think),* exhibited some thirty years ago at a provincial exhibition, which seemed instinct with Hogarthian humour, and painted with the knowledge and vigour of that great master. Moreover, I have seen upon his easel canvasses of far larger size, upon which the fairy world of Shakespeare was depicted with a kindred felicity of imagination. From his youth up it had been a subject of regret that the exigencies of early life had prevented him retaining that place on the bench of the Academy for which he had successfully fought; and later on, the sight of Raphael's cartoons filled him with shame at his own deficiencies. Like Sir Joshua when gazing on the same masterpieces, he felt that in art he must again "become as a little child"; and at the age of sixty-four, with the pluck of Cato the Censor who began Greek at seventy, he once more betook himself to the schools, and copied from the antique with all the ardour of a youth. By and by, falling more completely out of the movement of the time, he had leisure to devote himself more completely to oil-painting, and began, when a septuagenarian, his *opus magnum*, his vast cartoon, "The Worship of Bacchus," measuring 13 feet 3 inches by 7 feet 8 inches, and containing more than a thousand figures. He had the honour of exhibiting this when completed before the Queen; and afterwards accompanied it on a lecturing tour through the provinces,—an expedition that resulted in a loss of some two thousand pounds,—when I listened with intense interest to his own exposition of the marvellous work.† This picture, with much dramatic power, skilful grouping and clever drawing, is yet too sketchy, too grotesque, too amorphous, to stand the test of criticism from a rigid art-point of view. But it is manifestly unjust so to judge it, and ignore its other claims to interest and admiration. Still, it must be admitted that it has much to offend; and it is probable

---

* Probably "Grimaldi being Shaved by a Girl," now in the Westminster Aquarium. See Catalogue (No. 49) and the long explanatory note.

† See the published lecture by the artist, *The Worship of Bacchus*; London, W. Tweedie, 1867.

that in a later day, as now, it will be regarded as a gigantic failure, the outcome of an enormous amount of misapplied and infructuous labour. This picture, painted in 1862, was presented to the National Gallery in 1869 by Mr. R. E. Lofft and other friends of the painter. It has been engraved; the artist himself outlining the figures, and Mr. H. Mottram completing the work.

IX.

A few words seem opportune here of Cruikshank's labours in the cause of Temperance. HEINE would have had a sword instead of a laurel-wreath laid upon his coffin, because he had been a brave soldier in the war of the liberation of humanity. CRUIKSHANK might claim a similar trophy,—in place of the broken palette which symbolized the "finis" of Hogarth,—for he too had been a hardy warrior, not, like the Hamburgh Jew, in the struggle against outworn creeds and effete ideas, but against our national vice, which he rightly esteemed to be the cause of nine-tenths of the poverty, misery, and crime we see around us.

It cannot be a matter of doubt that by his devotion to this cause, art and his own fortunes suffered together. A man of his simplicity and thoroughness of character could hardly embrace a cause like this,—and there is none nobler—without a devotedness which the world is apt to term fanaticism. He was a man of a single eye, and could not serve two masters. Moreover his style suffered by the contraction of his ideas and sympathies, and his art became associated with that vulgarity and want of æstheticism which, perhaps necessarily, characterises the movement. More than this, some of his earliest friends were alienated, and remunerative work that might have been his was diverted, from sheer prejudice, into other hands.

X.

But if it should appear necessary to seek a cause for the retire ment of an octogenarian from active labour, another and more legitimate explanation may be given for George Cruikshank's partial disseverance from art during the last decade of his life. The

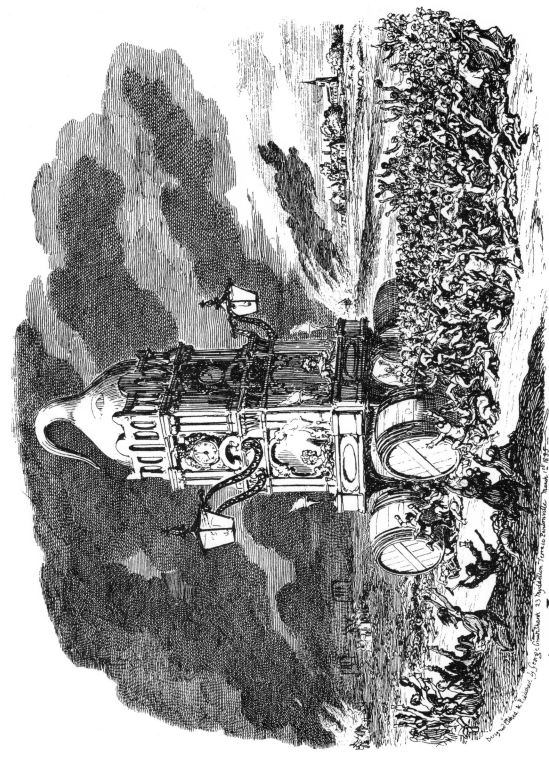

The GIN-JUGGARNATH. Or, The Worship of the GREAT SPIRIT of the age
— Its Devotees destroy themselves — It's progress is marked with desolation misery and Crime

most superficial study of the literature of Fiction, as it has been
cultivated during the past hundred years, will not fail to show us
that its aims, tendencies, and character have undergone a complete
change. The ludicrous situation, the comic adventure, the broad
joke, the coarse humour, which animate the pages of Fielding,
Smollett and Goldsmith, would be thought low and vulgar in these
days of hyperæsthetical refinement. Facilities of travelling and
inter-communication, cheap literature, and popular art, have gone
far to obliterate the distinctions of class, of insularity, and of pro-
vincialism. You shall find a Dodo as readily as a Parson Trulliber ;
and Squire Western, Commodore Trunnion, Philosopher Square
and Doctor Primrose are as completely extinct as the Mastodon
and the Ichthyosaurus. But if the more external and salient
features of humanity have undergone assimilation, there is still a
field for the masters and mistresses of fiction in the analysis of the
mental and moral nature. Subtle differentiation of character, nice
discrimination of motive, the ever insoluble problem—to man at
least—of femineity, the complexities arising from the sexual
relations,—all these are the farrago of the modern novelist, and
make altogether different demands upon illustrative art. Thus,
while the healthy manly humour of Charles Dickens in his early
works found in George Cruikshank its most felicitous exponent,
other collaboration was advisedly sought for the sickly pathos and
the mannered twaddle which the novelist gave us as his own attempt
to accommodate his style to the literary movement. It is not that
the art, the taste, the morality, the social conditions, the manners
of his age were necessarily inferior to those of the present day—
they were merely different. It was these which the artist had out-
lived ; not his genius, nor himself.

XI.

It appears to me that in any account of George Cruikshank, however imperfect, some notice must necessarily be given to the brother,
with whom, in his early art-life, he was associated, and for some
period even identified. Isaac Robert—or, as he is generally
called, Robert—Cruikshank, was just three years older than his

now more celebrated brother. The father, old Isaac Cruikshank, had not met with such encouragement in art as to lead to a desire to bring his elder son up to his own profession; and the mother, a sailor's daughter, had maritime proclivities. Hence the lad was sent as midshipman on E.I.C.'s vessel "Perseverance," where he remained for some time. At length, returning home and finding that Gillray, Woodward, Bunbury, and Dighton had vanished from the scene,—that Rowlandson was growing old, fat, and careless,—and that his brother George was beginning to get fair employment,—he, too, determined to adopt art, for which he had an inherited talent, as a profession. His age enabled him to take the upper hand; indeed, as a draughtsman, he was thought to be the cleverer fellow of the two, and many a plate, like "The Sparring Match at the Fives Court," in Pierce Egan's *Boxiana*, was etched by George from a design by his elder brother. At this time it was the intention of the pair to establish themselves as miniature painters—Robert being the draughtsman* and George the colourist—"the putter in of the sublime"—as the former would laughingly term it. But this idea was never fully carried out, and the brothers soon found remunerative employment in the field of political and social caricature. We have seen how they were associated in Pierce Egan's *Life in London*, and how George's retirement from the engagement, in disapprobation of the tendency of the work, left Robert master of the field. For William Hone the latter worked as well as his brother. In 1815 he drew the portrait of Elizabeth Fenning, for Hone's *Report of the Trial* of that unfortunate victim of circumstantial evidence. Like George, too, he took either side in the Caroline contest. For Dolby of the Strand he illustrated *The New Royal Game of Chess;* the *Political All-My-Knack for the Year of our Lord 1821; The Queen and Magna Charta, or the Thing that John signed; The Total Eclipse, a Grand Politico-Astronomical Phenomenon, 1820*, and others; for Effingham Wilson *A Peep at the P * v * * * * n, or Boiled Mutton with Caper Sauce at the*

---

* "My brother, Isaac Robert," says George, in a letter to Mr. Reid, "was a very clever miniature and portrait painter, and also a designer and etcher." There was unavoidable rivalry and jealousy between the two men, and their habits and characters were incongruous; but George always spoke of his old associate with tender affection, and further on, in the letter I have quoted from, alludes to his "dear brother Robert."

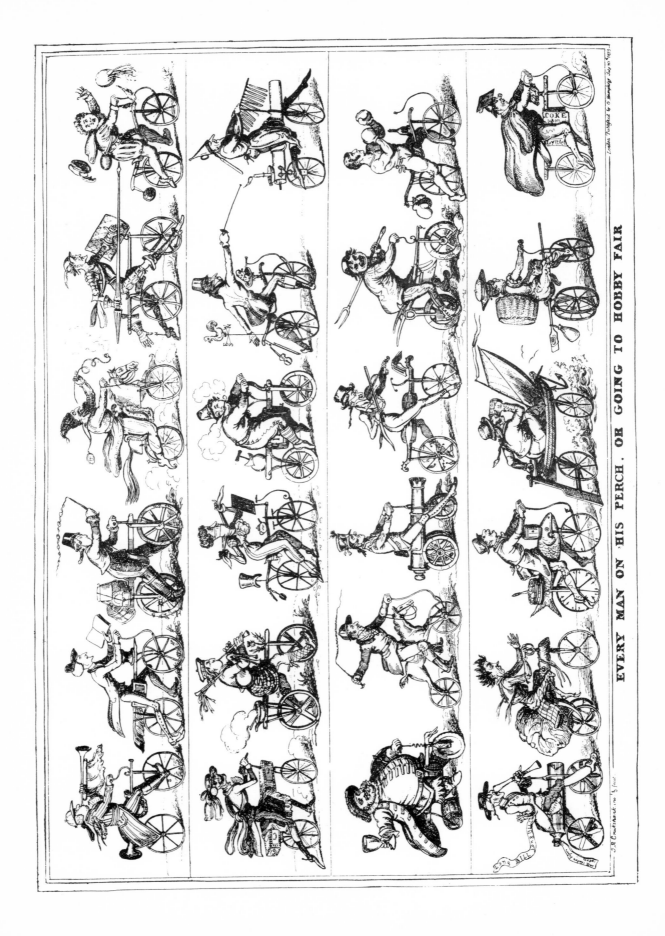

EVERY MAN ON HIS PERCH, OR GOING TO HOBBY FAIR

Temple of Joss, 1820; for Dean and Munday *The Men in the Moon, or the Devil to Pay;* and he as well as George—though not in unison—contributed designs of a more serious character to Nightingale's *Memoirs of Queen Caroline,* a bulky octavo, published by J. Robins in 1820.

A very spirited etching, 16in. by 11in., published by G. Humphrey July 10, 1819, merits special attention. It is inscribed : "Every Man on his Perchr, or Going to Hobby Fair." Half a century before, Ferguson, the astronomer, had told Dr. Johnson of "a new invented machine which went without horses—a man who sat in it turned a handle which worked a spring that drove it forward." "Then, sir," replied the Doctor, "what is gained is, the man has his choice whether he will move himself alone, or himself and the machine too." The laborious vehicle became obsolete, but at the period of the publication of this plate it was re-invented, and every "dandy" had his "hobby-horse," an instrument with either two or three wheels,—no crank or treadles,—and requiring propulsion by the impact of the riders' feet upon the ground. In one of Hone's curious and scarce publications, *The Age of Intellect, or Clerical Show-Folk and Wonderful Lay-Folk.* By Francis Moore, Physician (London, 1819, 8vo.) there is a curious coloured frontispiece by *George* Cruikshank, on which, among other wonders of the day, we see one dandy painfully struggling up-hill on his bicycle, and another, who, rushing precipitately down the too *facilis descensus,* is in the act of performing an involuntary summersault over his runaway carriage. The following lines in the book make allusion to the

> "—— patent pedestrian accelerators,
> The fleeting Velocipedes—Perambulators—
> Or Hobbies—which so much at present the rage are,
> That *asses* they'll banish from Brighton I'll wager."
>
> Page 171.

This is the fashion ridiculed in Robert's plate, where, in four parallel rows, we find represented twenty-four riders on Velocipedes,—the dress of the former indicating their professions or trades, and the latter appropriate to, or indicative of, the same by some peculiarity of construction. Thus the sailor sits in a *boat ;* the fiddler is astride on a *violin ;* the soldier is mounted on a *cannon;* the tallow-chandler bestrides a huge *candle;* and the apothecary is bifurcated by one of his own labelled phials. The plate is rare and equally clever in design and execution. There is also before me a smaller etching by the same hand, inscribed "Going to Hobby Fair," where we see a worthy cit of the Gilpin type transcending Johnson, for he is not only moving himself and the machine, but his wife and children into the bargain!

In 1820, we have *Lessons of Thrift published for the General Benefit, by a Member of the Save-all Club,* containing eleven clever coloured full-page etchings; in 1821, a quarto volume, handsomely printed by Bulmer, *Tales of the Cordelier Metamorphosed* (by G. Hibbert); and in 1824, *The Life and Exploits of Don Quixote,* "illustrated by 24 designs by Cruikshank" (Knight and Lacey, 1824, 2 vols. 8vo.) The designs are cut on wood, full-page size, and do not rise above mediocrity.

Several large folio-size etchings, in the Gillray style, by Robert Cruikshank, will be found in the collection of which I have spoke in a former page, entitled "Cruikshankiana." Among these may be mentioned one inscribed "Dandy Fainting, or an Exquisite in Fits;" "The *Broom* Sold," (a hit at Lord Brougham); "Household Troops," (a caricature of domestic servants); "Monstrosities of 1827," (a Satire on the Fashions); and "A Tea-Party, or English Manners and French Politeness."

I next lay my hand on a rare piece entitled *Mock Heroics, or Snuff, Tobacco, and Gin, and a Rhapsody on an Inkstand, with four appropriate caricature engravings by Cruikshank,* (1822) from the last three lines of which we gain the unexceptionable moral :—

> "Enjoy the gifts of Heaven in moderation,
> And then nor SNUFF, TOBACCO, GIN, nor recreation,
> Will in the least endanger your salvation."

In 1822—25 appeared an important serial work, now of considerable scarcity and value :—*Annals of Sporting and Fancy Gazette : a Magazine of Sporting Subjects and Fancy Pursuits.* This is illustrated with numerous coloured plates by R. Cruikshank, H. Alken, Egerton, &c.

As George published in 1823 his *Points of Humour,** so Robert

---

* George regarded this as an "imitation" of his own work, and felt it necessary to announce "that he did not make a single drawing for it." The following "Notice" also

in the same year produced twenty clever designs for woodcuts to illustrate *Points of Misery, or Fables for Mankind, Prose and Verse, chiefly original*, by Charles Westmacott ;* of which there were a hundred copies with proof impressions of the plates. By the same author, under the pseudonym of " Bernard Blackmantle," is a very curious and important book, *The English Spy, an original work, Characteristic, Satirical, and Humourous, Comprising Scenes and Sketches in every rank of Society, being Portraits of the Illustrious, Eminent, Eccentric and Notorious,* (2 vols. 8vo., 1825.) In the pages of these extraordinary volumes figure all the notabilities of the day, either openly, or under slight disguise ; and Tom Best, White-headed Bob, " Pea-green " Hayne, Pierce Egan, Colonel Berkeley, the " Golden Ball," " Horse " Kett, Beau Brummell, Charles Matthews, Jemmy Gordon, and a host of others of equal notoriety, mingle, cheek-by-jowl, in the vivid and moving panorama. The seventy-two large coloured plates are almost all by Robert Cruikshank, and include two by the veteran, Rowlandson. Portraits of the author are liberally introduced, and we find him especially in one of the admirable vignettes† on wood—the last in the book— where " Bob Transit," his companion, is a likeness of the artist. In this year, too, the latter furnished the large folding and other coloured plates for the second edition of Pierce Egan's *Sporting Anecdotes*.

In the following year (1826) we have the *The Punster's Pocket-Book; or the Art of Punning enlarged. By Bernard Blackmantle.* Some of the wood-cuts in this pretty volume, which is a *rifacimento* of the *Ars Punica* of Dr. Sheridan, as enlarged by Swift, are worthy, in spirit and delicacy, of George himself.

---

appeared at the same time :—" As there are works continually advertised, ' *with plates by Cruikshank*,' the Public are particularly requested to observe that *George* Cruikshank has no connexion with any Publications to which his Christian Name is not affixed ; and that all Works, for which he has made designs, are advertised with his name in full."

* Charles Molloy Westmacott, a natural son of the celebrated sculptor whose name he assumed, was a typical editor of the " rowdy " period of journalism. He conducted the *Age* newspaper, and wrote the *Annual Critical Catalogue to the Royal Academy.* Charles Kemble horsewhipped him in 1830 for an alleged insult to his daughter Fanny, and Bulwer threatened a like procedure, but did not carry it out. He retired to Paris, where he died in 1868.

† There is an exquisite wood-cut on the title page which I find a difficulty in attributing to either of the artists,—Cruikshank, Gillray, Rowlandson, and Finlay—to whom the vignettes are assigned. It illustrates the distich

" By Frolic, Mirth, and Fancy gay,
Old Father Time is borne away

—and is worthy of Bartolozzi or Cipriani.

In 1827 the two brothers once more collaborated in the illustration of a charming volume, entitled *London Characters,* which now holds place in the estimation of collectors among the rarest and most covetable in the entire kyriell of Cruikshankiana. This was published by Robins, and contains twenty-four coloured plates, of which *nine* are by Robert Cruikshank, and the remaining fifteen by his brother George, among whose more admirable productions they are justly reckoned. It is in 12mo. ; and a fine copy would probably realize " paper." Robert contributed three illustrations also in this year to the *Fairy Tales,* from the German of Albert Ludwig Grimm, the remaining cuts being from the pencil of his brother George.

In 1828 appeared *Doings in London, or Day and Night Scenes of the Frauds, Frolics, Manners, and Depravities of the Metropolis.* This book, which was written by George Smeeton, the printer, contains a large amount of really curious antiquarian information, and is illustrated by twenty-three very characteristic designs, cut on wood by Bonner. By Smeeton also was published *The British Dance of Death, exemplified by a Series of Engravings from Drawings by Van Assen,* for which Robert produced the admirable coloured frontispiece, exhibiting in compartments the doings of the King of Terrors, who, seated in the midst, with crowned head and scythe, manipulates the globe which acknowledges his sway. In this year, too, was published *The Spirit of the Age Newspaper for 1828,* the bastard title-page of which is adorned with a charming vignette on wood by Bonner, which bears the name of our artist as designer ; and *The Universal Songster, or Museum of Mirth, forming the most complete, extensive, and valuable Collection of Ancient and Modern Songs in the English Language, Amatory, Bucchanalian, Comic, Masonic, Naval, Sporting, &c.* (3 vols, 8vo.), with humourous characteristic frontispieces, and 87 wood-cuts designed by George and Robert Cruikshank. We find also by the latter thirteen coloured plates in *London Oddities, or Theatrical Cabinet, Tit Bits of Humour and Eccentricity.*

Now comes the *Finish to the Adventures of Tom, Jerry, and Logic in their Pursuits through Life in and out of London.* By Pierce Egan, (1830,) with its thirty-six coloured " Scenes from Real

Life," and clever wood-cut vignettes, all the work of Robert Cruikshank. Of this volume I have already spoken at length on page 24.

A series of little books published about this time by Kidd, Miller, and others, which have been since collected together in two volumes, and issued under the common title of *Facetiæ: Being a general collection of the Jeux d' Esprits, which have been illustrated by Robert Cruikshank*, contain some of the choicest and most characteristic specimens of his talent. Among them we have Dibdin's *High Mettled Racer*,* *Monsieur Nongtongpaw*, Taylor's *Monsieur Tonson, Margate*, Pierce Egan's *Snuff-box and the Leetel Bird*, Moncrieff's *March of Intellect*, and *Old Booty*, Montagu's *Monsieur Mallet*, Coleridge's *Devil's Walk, The Devil's Visit, The Real Devil's Walk, Brighton*, and *Steamers and Stages.* In similar form we have also, *Walks about Town by an Antiquated Trio, The condition of the West Indian Slave contrasted with that of the Infant Slave in our English Factories, Trip to Greenwich Fair, Cruikshank and the New Police, Cruikshank versus Witchcraft, Mary Ogilvy, Wee Watty*, and *Robert Cruikshank versus Sir Andrew Agnew ;* to which may be added from Thomas's "Comic Drama," Foote's *Tailors, a Tragedy for Warm Weather*, Kane O'Hara's *Midas, a Burletta*, Foote's *Mayor of Garratt*, Gay's *Beggar's Opera*, and Shakespeare's *Katherine and Petruchio.*

The admirable designs in these charming little volumes, which should find a place in every Cruikshankian collection, are variously cut on wood by Bonner, Byfield, Kirchner, S. Williams, Sears, Slader, Walker, and Robert's son, Percy Cruikshank.

When George published his *Comic Alphabet*, Robert was not long in "following suit." I have before me *The Comic Alphabet, containing Twenty-six illustrations by Cruikshank*, by W. R. Macdonald. The designs are circular, well cut on wood, and in spirit and force worthy of the rival artist.

In 1831 was published by Moxon that exquisite piece of humour, *Satan in Search of a Wife, with the whole Process of his Courtship and Marriage, and who danced at the Wedding. By an Eye-Witness.* This "eye-witness" was no other than Charles Lamb, whose

---

* Southey (*Colloquies* I. 326.) said of this ballad that "it ought to be printed in every spelling-book, and learnt by heart in every nursery."

ovine turn of thought is discernible in every stanza. It is excessively rare, and although one of the happiest and most characteristic productions of the man, has not been included in any collection of "Eliana." I can hardly venture to assert that the clever cuts by Bonner are from the pencil of Robert Cruikshank; but I do not know to whom I may otherwise attribute them.

In 1834 appeared a very elegant volume : *Original Fables, with Morals and Ethical Index, written by Job Crithannah, embellished with an elaborate frontispiece and eighty-four original designs by* R. Cruickshank (*sic*), engraved on wood by Slader, Dodd, Williams, Bonner, and others,—the author's real name being, I believe, Nathan Birch. In 1836, we have : *Readings from Dean Swift, His " Tale of a Tub," with Variorum Notes, and a Supplement. For the use of the Nineteenth Century. By Quinbus Flestrin Grildrig,* with six hard and coarsely executed wood-cuts ; in 1838, *Divine Emblems,* by Johann Abricht, **A.M.** ; in 1839, *The Lady and the Saints,* with ten vignettes on wood ; in 1843, *Tales and Legends of the Isle of Wight.* By Abraham Elder, with fourteen etchings, of very careless and indifferent character (originally published without the illustrations in *Bentley's Miscellany*) ; in 1843, *Chronicles of the Bastille,* with 40 plates ; and in 1849, *The Orphan, or Memoirs of Matilda* by Eugène Sue, translated by the Hon. D. G. Osborne, with 24 illustrations. Without date, but a few years earlier, we have the *Hudibrastic History of Lord Amherst's Visit to China,* by W. A. Kentish, "with a Parody of God Save the King" ; Kidd's *London Directory and London Ambulator ;* Kidd's *Golden Key of the Treasures of Knowledge,* and the *Little World of Great and Good Things ;* and *Cruikshank's Offering of Mirth.*

For George Daniel, of Canonbury Square, Islington, the sale of whose extraordinary collection in 1864 constitutes an epoch in the annals of bibliography, our artist, in conjunction with John Leech, illustrated with etchings *Merrie England in the Olden Time,* a book containing no small amount of curious antiquarian information, drawn from the marvellous literary stores of the author. The original issue of 1841 has become very scarce, but a cheap reprint can now be obtained from Messrs. Warne and Co.

With the same George Daniel as editor, and R. W. Buss and T.

Wageman as artists, he was associated in the illustration of Cumberland's *British and Minor Theatre*, the publishers of which describe his designs as "prominent scenes, excellently well engraved by Bonner, from drawings sketched in the Theatre by the celebrated and eccentric Robert Cruikshank, than whom, in the delineation of mirth, mischief, extravagance and whim, a more cunning wight never wielded pencil or brush."

The collector will hardly neglect the acquisition of three amusing volumes entitled *Cruikshank at Home*, with their full-page woodcuts and numerous clever vignettes. These were supplemented by *The Odd Volume, or Book of Variety ; illustrated by two odd fellows, Seymour and Cruikshank.* In the Preface to this we read that the "Engravings are the joint production of *two* clever artists—the one, Mr. Cruikshank, a long-established favourite,—the other, Mr. Seymour, a gentleman of far superior talent, but hitherto, perhaps, not quite so extensively known, in consequence of his short residence in London." We get further bibliographical information in a note :—

"These designs were originally intended for a fourth volume of CRUIKSHANK AT HOME ; but in consequence of the late disagreement between the two brothers Cruikshank (in reference to the question, 'Which is *the real* SIMON PURE ?') the projected title has been changed, and the work, by the assistance of Mr. Seymour, metamorphosed into an '*Odd*' Volume."

Hereby hangs a curious story, of which I am reminded as I write. When a certain ingenious German writer, Herr Nagler, compiling a *Kunstler's Lexicon*, came to draw up a notice of George Cruikshank, his eye was caught, in looking over some English review, by the statement, in answer to the question cited above, that "the real Simon Pure was George Cruikshank." The formula, become proverbial among ourselves, was not familiar to him, and he took it to mean that the latter was an *assumed* name and the former the *real* one. He accordingly commenced his biography thus,—"PURE (Simon), the real name of the celebrated caricaturist, George Cruikshank," &c. !

The fact is, George, who was not improperly tenacious of his own merits and reputation, had, since his professional severance from his brother, suffered much annoyance from the dishonesty of certain publishers, who sought, by the omission of the Christian name, to impose upon the public as his designs those of the elder and less able artist. Years after, when poor Robert had departed "ad plures," there was still a second "Cruikshank" to claim a share of the honour and rewards associated with the name. Thus George thought it "a duty" to inform the public that he had a nephew whose Christian name was "Percy,"—that he was employed by "a person of the name of Read,"—that the latter, in advertising any work executed by the nephew, announced it "as by 'Cruikshank,' " and that numerous persons, he was informed, had purchased such publications under the impression that they were illustrated by himself. He therefore cautioned the public against buying any work as his with the name of Read, of Johnson's Court, upon it as publisher,—that he "never did anything for that person and never should,"—and that his "observations" were not directed against his nephew, to whom he wished every good, but against the said Read, who by leaving out the Christian name of the latter had deprived him of his just credit, and created a "confusion of persons which if not done for the purpose of deceiving the public, appears to be very much like it." The King, however, never dies ; and of late years we have had a *second* "George Cruikshank," a son of the aforesaid Percy, (who, by the way, besides being a designer, was a skilful engraver on wood, and cut many of his uncle's and father's designs). This second George, during the life-time of his great uncle, very properly appended "Junior" to his signature, or styled himself "Calvert" Cruikshank, from the name of his mother, a daughter of an artist of considerable talent, formerly resident in Birmingham. Thus, when in 1875, he illustrated for Messrs. Grant and Co. a *History of Bluebeard's Wives*, he styled himself on the title-page "George Cruikshank Junior." It was this probably that incited the authorities of the British Museum to describe *the* George Cruikshank as "the elder," on every occurrence of his name in their Catalogue,—a precaution which may possibly lead to the attribution to old Isaac himself of some of the works of his gifted son ; and, in a future day, to still further "confusion of persons," when the collector, puzzled by so many "Richmonds in the field,"

may have difficulty in discriminating between these various representatives of four generations of comic artists. I need only add that of this "younger" George I possess, or have seen, designs of considerable merit, and that he seems likely to sustain worthily the reputation of the name. Still, the practised eye will distinguish the "GEORGIUM SIDUS" from its satellites,—alike now and to the end of time, to the connoisseur, there can be but ONE George Cruikshank.

But before I bid farewell to ROBERT, a parting word remains to be said. I have hitherto spoken only of his book-illustrations, which were too often hasty, slovenly, and uninformed by that earnest and conscientious spirit which characterized every thing to which the younger brother put his hand. They were in fact "pot-boilers," and were so regarded by the careless artist. But the same cannot be said of the exquisitely finished water-colour drawings which he occasionally made for private patrons, and by which his capabilities may be more fairly judged. Here, says one who knew him long and well,—the late George Daniel, of Islington, his literary coadjutor in *Cumberland's British Theatre* :—" His genius is advantageously seen. He was apt to conceive and prompt to execute. He had a quick eye and a ready hand. With all his extravagant drollery, his drawing is anatomically correct ; his details are minute, expressive, and of careful finish ; and his colouring is bright and delicate. The best efforts of Gillray and Rowlandson may hardly compare with them. Of these choice specimens there were, unhappily, but few. He could afford neither time nor study to produce them unless a patron came forth, and then their production was his especial delight." In private life, he was a man of considerable reading, fluent conversation, gentlemanly manners, and liberal hospitality. He had much of the carelessness of genius, and a disposition to indulge too freely in the pleasures of the table. The favorite amusement of his leisure hours was archery. He was an ardent toxophilite ; and had acquired such skill in the use of the bow that in the days gone by he would hardly have been deemed an "vnperfyte shoter" by old Ascham himself, or failed to cleave the willow-wand in the glades of merry Sherwood. He had known, as well as drawn, " each shade of many coloured life " ; and had experienced one and the other fortune. His chequered career came to a close on March 13th, 1856, when he died, after a short illness, of bronchitis, in the 66th year of his age   "An eminent artist, a facetious companion, and a kindly man has just passed away,"—wrote his ancient ally, George Daniel, in a short but feeling tribute to the memory of his old acquaintance, in his little volume *Love's Last Labour Not Lost,* (London, Pickering, 1863), p. 163.   He left a son, Percy, alluded to above as a designer, but better known by his more legitimate profession of an engraver on wood.   In this capacity he executed, as we have seen, some of the

(From an Original Pencil Drawing.)

engravings from his father's designs ; and a vignette engraved by him from a drawing by his uncle, George, will be found in a curious volume entitled *Martin's Vagaries ; being the sequel to " A*

Tale of a Tub," recently discovered at the University of Oxford. *Edited with Notes by Scriblerus Oxoniensis.* (London, 1843, 8vo),—in which are also two full-page etchings, signed " George Cruikshank."

I do not pretend to have written a life, or anything approaching to an exhaustive bibliography, of Robert Cruikshank. All that I have attempted to do is to put together some trivial *mémoires pour servir*, by indicating from the materials before me, some noteworthy points in his career as an artist. To accomplish this much appeared desirable for the following reasons :—I have never seen any account of him, and am not aware that any exists ; he was a draughtsman of considerable talent, and supremely typical of his interesting period ; he was the early associate of the immortal George, and the work of the two men is, in some cases, indistinguishable ; he is unwisely, as it appears to me, ignored and neglected by collectors ; and lastly, because, in my opinion, the *par nobile fratrum* should be associated by their works, through all time, in the same portfolio.

As it is. I may be thought to have indulged in too long an *excursus,* and must return to the " SIMON PURE " of the present essay.

XII.

We all know the story of the pedant of Hierocles, who, wishing to sell his house, carried about with him a brick as a specimen. In the analysis of his art-work which I have attempted, I have, of course, found it necessary to particularize ; but it is by no such procedure that an adequate estimate can be formed of the genius of George Cruikshank. This must be guaged, not by a few master-pieces, as in the case of some great artists, but by the entire range and aggregate of his productions. " Look at one of his works," as Thackeray well puts it, " and we pronounce him an excellent humourist ; look at all, his reputation is increased by a kind of geometrical progression,—as a whole diamond is a hundred times more valuable than the hundred splinters into which it might be broken.' And, whether we regard it collectively or in detail, what an enormous mass of admirable work is the outcome of these well-nigh four score years of earnest, honest, single-minded labour ! He was a man of unflagging industry, inexhaustible invention, and the utmost facility of execution. His life, as he himself once described it to me, had been as that of a squirrel in its cage,—paddling with his hands, as he spoke, to suggest the monotonous action of the little animal. Thus the mere number of his productions is something prodigious. Mr. Reid has registered nearly 5,000 separate designs, though his *Catalogue* stops at the year 1870; and the largest known collection, that of Mr. Edward Truman, of 23, Old Burlington Street, contains over 7,000. Yet when we reflect that the art-work of JOHN LEECH, extending over a period of not more than five and twenty years, represents a totality of 5,000 designs, we are forced to the conclusion that even these collections are comparatively insignificant and incomplete. Indeed, I should myself have hazarded the supposition that George Cruikshank must have altogether produced not less than from 15,000 to 20,000 separate pieces.

Here may once more be suggested the problem, which I shall not now attempt to solve, whether the artist suffers a dynamical loss in direct ratio with the numerical increase of his productions. Thackeray's metaphor hardly runs on all fours; for after all, the diamond *has been* broken into splinters, and its market value can never more be the same. Again, the old question as to what constitutes " High Art,"—so well answered by Charles Lamb,—may still be put, legitimately enough, by those who are so constituted as not to receive elevated or agreeable impressions from a certain class of subjects, and to whom a primrose is but a primrose, however glorified by art.* For my own part, I must confess, that in the intense gratification which I have derived from the study of the productions of George Cruikshank, it never occurred to me, as a matter to be regretted, that he had not employed his genius in a different direction. But such a regret has been felt, and expressed in exquisite language, by a critic whose purity of sentiment and eloquence of diction always captivate the soul, even where his reasoning fails to convince the understanding. Without venturing to express an opinion of my own on a subject where so much might be said, I conclude this section with the passage I refer to :

---

* " A Primrose by a river's brim,
 A yellow primrose was to him,
 And it was nothing more."
    —WORDSWORTH, *Peter Bell*

—" Among the foremost men whose power has had to assert itself, though with contest, yet with countless loss, through peculiarly English disadvantages of circumstance, are assuredly to be ranked together, both for honour and for mourning, Thomas Bewick and George Cruikshank. There is, however, less cause for regret in the instance of Bewick. We may understand that it was well for us once to see what an entirely powerful painter's genius, and an entirely keen and true man's temper, could achieve together, unhelped, but also unharmed, among the black banks and wolds of Tyne. But the genius of Cruikshank has been cast away in an utterly ghastly and lamentable manner : his superb line-work, worthy of any class of subject, and his powers of conception and composition, of which I cannot venture to estimate the range in their degraded application, having been condemned by his fate, to be spent either in rude jesting, or in vain war with conditions of vice too low alike for record or rebuke, among the dregs of the British populace. Yet perhaps I am wrong in regretting even this : it may be an appointed lesson for futurity that the art of the best English etcher in the nineteenth century, spent on illustrations of the lives of burglars and drunkards, should one day be seen in museums beneath Greek vases fretted with drawings of the wars of Troy, or side by side with Dürer's ' Knight and Death.' " *

XIII.

It may appear strange that an artist of such amazing energy of productiveness,—his name a household word in our homes,—and his work giving popularity and value to anything with which it was associated,—should not have accumulated wealth for himself as well as for others. But the explanation is not far to seek. " Of all arts and professions in this country," writes Thomas Keightley in the amusingly egotistical preface to his *Fairy Mythology,* " that of literature is the least respected and the worst remunerated." This might have been asserted with even more truth of comic art,—at least during the period of George's greatest fecundity. " He has

---

*The Queen of the Air, being a Study of the Greek Myths of Cloud and Storm. By John Ruskin, L.L.D., London, 1869, 8vo, p. 161.

been obliged to sell his wit for his bread, week by week," say Thackeray, " to wring laughter day by day, sometimes, perhaps, out of want, often certainly from ill-health or depression,—to keep the fire of his brain perpetually alight, for the greedy public will give it no leisure to cool ; " and the same author adds, " time was (we are told so in print) when for a picture with thirty heads in it he was paid three guineas—a poor week's pittance truly, and a dire week's labour ! " For the designs for Hone's Political squibs I have heard that the artist's ordinary remuneration was half a guinea each only. Mr. Sala, a very competent authority, states that he was, " as a rule, very poorly paid,"—that for an illustrative etching on a plate octavo-size he never received more than twenty-five pounds, and had been paid as low as ten,—that he had often drawn "a charming little vignette on wood" for a guinea,—and questions whether his average income, taking the bad years with the good, exceeded six hundred pounds a year. But besides that he lived before the days of liberal art-remuneration, he was of an open, trustful disposition, gave and lent freely, kept a respectable establishment, and had, moreover, sustained heavy losses in certain enterprizes connected with his profession. Thus, years ago, Thackeray had felt it necessary to ask if there was " no way in which the country could acknowledge the long services and brave career of such a friend and benefactor,"—of this " fine rough English diamond," as he termed him. But nothing was done ; and a new generation came on who knew not George,—or knowing him, regarded him as already belonging to the past. Thus, when in 1866, a committee, with JOHN RUSKIN at its head, sought to give a practical answer to the question by the collection of a " Subscription Testimonial," the attempt was a failure, hundreds only being received when thousands were expected. It is, however, a consolation to know that the honourable poverty of this distinguished man was, in some measure, alleviated by a pension of £100 from the Civil List, on the ground of his public services as an artist ; and that this, by the direction of the Earl of Beaconsfield, is continued to his respected widow. He also enjoyed a pension of £50 from the Royal Academy's "Turner" Annuities.

With this slender *viaticum* for the evening of that day whose

The Rose and the Lily

morning-march had been so worthily and independently accomplished, the artist approached the conclusion of his ninth decade. So late as last year was published Mrs. Octavian Blewitt's *Rose and Lily, how they became the Emblems of England and France, a Fairy Tale,* containing a frontispiece "Designed and etched by George Cruikshank, age 83—1875"—probably the last book illustrated by his hand; and only a few months ago his name was subscribed to a letter in the *Times,* concerning the statue of Bruce for the battle-field of Bannockburn, of which he claimed to be the designer,—his last appearance before the public. Retaining, even in this advanced age, much of the vivacity of temperament, the sprightliness of fancy, the warmth of heart, and the cheerfulness of disposition which had characterized him through life, he seemed to realize Sir Walter Scott's beautiful description of King René :—

> "A mirthful man he was; the snows of age
> Fell, but they did not chill him. Gaiety,
> Even in life's closing, touched his teeming brain
> With such wild visions as the setting sun
> Raises in front of some hoar glacier,
> Painting the bleak ice with a thousand hues."

Of a fine constitution, active habits,* and that type of bodily conformation which seemed to promise longevity, he bade fair to furnish an example of centenarianism in which even the sagacity of a THOMS could find no flaw. But alas! though Art is immortal, the Artist dies,—

> "——————— nec pietas moram
> Rugis, et instanti senectæ
> Afferet, indomitæque morti."

Early in this year GEORGE CRUIKSHANK was attacked by bronchitis —the same malady which just at this period carried off two honoured veterans in literature—PROFESSOR CREASY and DOCTOR DORAN. He made successful battle against the disease, and hopes were entertained of his final recovery. But this was not to be;

---

* Nearly seventy years ago, he served as private in the Loyal North British Volunteers. The establishment of the Volunteer force afforded him, in 1859, an opportunity of again displaying his military ardour. He joined the Havelock, or 48th Middlesex Rifle Corps,— all, by the way, total abstainers,—of which he became Lieutenant Colonel. This post he continued to hold in spite of the expressed opinion of his officers that he was, from his great age, incompetent for the duties of the position. A memorial on the subject was sent to the Lord Lieutenant, and by him forwarded to the War Office. The result was an order, in an., 1869, to cashier every one of the fourteen officers who had signed the document. Then the regiment was left with three or four officers only,—an octogenarian commander and the rest mere lads. His own resignation followed.

and on Feb. 1, 1878, a universal feeling of sorrow was occasioned by the intelligence that the great master who had lived in the reigns of four English monarchs, and delighted by his art as many successive generations of men, had passed away from among us. A noble appeal was made in the columns of the *Daily Telegraph* by his old friend MR. SALA, for a sepulchre in St. Paul's; but this, from actual want of space in the crypt could not, at the time, be accorded. So, on the following Saturday, his honoured remains were borne* to a resting place at Kensall Green, amid the regrets of the few who loved him for his noble nature, the many who knew him but by his art, and a host of fellow-workers in the great harvest-field of Temperance.

XIV.

ERE in conclusion, I may venture to express in brief and hasty summary the opinion which personal knowledge and loving study have led me to form of GEORGE CRUIKSHANK, in the threefold aspect in which I have sought to exhibit him :—

As a MAN, few have led so pure and blameless a life as he; or left behind a name and reputation so altogether unsmirched. Honourable, truthful, generous, unselfish, open, warm-hearted, and single-minded, he retained to the last day of his long and noble life, the wit of a man with the simplicity of a child. Mixing freely with the miserable, the profligate and the vicious of mankind, he was "among them, but not of them;" familiar from his boyhood with the metropolitan dens of misfortune, infamy, and crime, he ever came out the purer from the contact. His singularly pure and healthy nature refused the assimilation of evil; or rather, like the Pontic monarch of olden days, he found wholesome nourishment in the very poison, and throve on that which would have been the death of a weaker nature. With an adequate conception of his own talents, and some jealousy as to their fitting recognition, he had yet much of the humility of true genius, and was generous in acknowledgement of the merits of others. He was fearless as

---

* The bearers were Lord Houghton (Moncton Milnes), Samuel Carter Hall, F.S,A. Charles Landseer, R.A., George Augustus Sala, Mr. Ellis, and General McMurdo.

Bayard in what he deemed to be right, and had the manliness and chivalry of nature of an ancient Paladin. In a century prolific to an extraordinary degree of remarkable men, he stands out one of the most noteworthy, typical, and interesting. He never made an enemy, and was beloved by his contemporaries of the successive generations through which he lived. " His friends," said the learned antiquary, the late Thomas Wright, "not only admire him for his talents, but love him for his kind and genial spirit;" and among these,—to adopt the words of the same accomplished writer—none loved and admired him more than he who now pens this imperfect tribute to his memory.

As a HUMOURIST,* it is his glory that by his example and influence he emancipated Comic Art from the grossness and vulgarity with which, till his day, it had been associated; raised it to the highest point to which it has yet attained;

---

* At the commencement of the present essay, I sought to characterise broadly, and yet definitely, the four artists whom I considered to be the cardinal representatives of the various branches of pictorial satire, as it has been practised in this country. But I by no no means expect that every art-critic will consider my choice judicious. It is the old difficulty :—

"Quid dem? quid non dem? renuis quod tu, jubet alter."

—An able and genial French writer, M. Ernest Chesneau, in a paper entitled, " Un Humoriste Anglais : John Leech," in the *Gazette des Beaux-Arts*, (1875, p. 532), places that artist in a higher rank than I, admirable as I admit his talents to be, should be disposed to concede to him ; and would, I doubt not, consider any generalization imperfect which did not include him as the typical head and representative of a class. As bearing upon Hogarth, George Cruikshank, and Satiric Art in England, the remarks of a critical foreigner will be read with interest, if not with entire concurrence :—

" Le nom de JOHN LEECH mérite de prendre place dans la mémoire de tous les amateurs auprès d'un autre nom justement célèbre, celui de WILLIAM HOGARTH.

" JOHN LEECH ne nous apparaît pas plus que WILLIAM HOGARTH comme un caricaturiste. Ils se servent l'un et l'autre du crayon ou de la brosse dans une fin étrangère á celle du rire qui est le but des déformations apportées á la réalité par la caricature. On sait quel terrible moraliste, quel satirique violent, cruel, implacable, fut ce grossier Saxon d' Hogarth, dont le génie amer, vigoureux, animé par une verve endiablée, fit hurler sous le fouet les laideurs, les infirmités, et les vices de ses contemporains. Il s'attaque aux monstruosités morales et pathologiques de son temps,—étroitement solidaires, celles-ci de celles-là,—avec l'emportement sanguin et la bileuse énergie d'une misanthropie indignée, révoltée dans tous ses instincts honnêtes. Hogarth est de la famille de Timon d'Athènes, une sorte d'Alceste trivial et brutal. * * * * " Chez JOHN LEECH, il faut le répéter, parceque e'est un trait caractéristique, la vieille rudesse anglaise s'est extrêmement adoucie, Je l'opposais à Hogarth au début de ces quelques pages : j'aurais pu étendre la comparaison et opposer son aimable philosophie aux violences, aux brutalités, aux grossiéretés, aux indécences, à l'âpreté, à l'ardeur de vengeance, au fiel, à la haine des caricaturistes anglais en ce siècle, du misérable GILLRAY, de BUNBURY, de SEYMOUR, d'ALKEN, de ROWLANDSON, et surtout de l'apostat CRUIKSHANK, dont les œuvres pleines d'imagination, de verve, de fougue, d'énergie, d'ardeur, de fantaisie, de trait, de caprice, sont à l'œuvre de Leech ce qu'une suite de furieuses invectives serait à la fine épigramme d'un galant homme et d'un lettré."

and did much to gain it the position which it ought to occupy :*
that he never transgressed the narrow line that separates wit from
buffoonery and vulgarity, pandered to sensuality, glorified vice, or
raised a laugh at the expence of decency. Satire, in his hands,
never degenerated into brutality or scurrility. A moral purpose
ever underlaid his humour ; he sought to instruct or improve when
he amused. " He has told us," finely says Thackeray, " a thousand
new truths in as many strange and fascinating ways ; he has given
a thousand new and pleasant thoughts to millions of people ; he
has never used his wit dishonestly ; he has never, in all the
exuberance of his frolicsome nature, caused a single painful or
guilty blush. How little do we think of the extraordinary power
of this man, and how ungrateful we are to him ! "

As an ARTIST, in his own special line, he is *primus absque
secundo ;*—" none but himself can be his parallel." He reigns
supreme and solitary in a clearing—so to speak—of his own ;
distinct, on the one hand, from the high park-lands of the
aristocracy of Art, and on the other, from the common sward of
the indiscriminate mob. With his talents, energy, and industry,
he might doubtless have done anything that any one had done
before him ; have made a name, had he so willed it, in Art
Religious or Historical, — in Portraiture, Landscape, Conversations, Animal or Still Life. But he instinctively took a
domain or walk of his own ; and having taken it, made it and
himself famous. Simple, intelligible, and popular in all that he
did, he had gained an impregnable lodgment in the hearts of the
people a generation before his merits as an artist proper had been
recognized by the critics.† His genius was strictly autochthonic ;

---

* That is, as a branch of the Fine Arts. Its importance in the domain of Archæology
has been sufficiently vindicated by Malcolm *(Historical Sketch of the Art of Caricaturing*
London, 1813, 4to) ; Panofka (*Parodien und Karikaturen auf Werken der Klassiken Kunst,*
Berlin, 1850, 8vo) ;) Wright *(A History of Caricature and Grotesque in Literature and Art,*
London, 1865, 4to) ; and Champfleury (*Histoire de la Caricature Antique et au Moyen-âge*
Paris, 1872, 2 vols., 12mo.)

† Among these may be cited an admirable artist and able critic, Mr. P. G. Hamerton,
whose well-considered judgment I should regret not to be able to place on record :—" There
is in CRUIKSHANK an artist within or behind the caricaturist ; and this artist is a person of
exceptional endowment. His invention is vivid, and his power of drawing the figures
invented is singularly sprightly and precise. There are etchings by CRUIKSHANK, though
these are not numerous in proportion to the mass of his great labours, which are as
excellent artistically as they are notable for genius and wit, where the stroke of the needle

he belonged to no School or Academy ; he held no diploma or titular distinction ; he had neither rival nor imitator ; and as he had no master, so he had no disciple,* and has left no successor.†
He was a man *sui generis ;* in British Art, like Jean Paul Richter in German literature, he is 𝔇𝔢𝔯 𝔊𝔦𝔫𝔷𝔦𝔤𝔢,—"the only one"; and of him, now that he has left us, it may be aptly said, as of another great humourist of a former day :—

> " Long shall we seek his likeness,—long in vain,
> And turn to all of him which may remain,
> Sighing that Nature form'd but one such man,
> And broke the die ——— ·————" ‡

XV.

𝔅𝔦𝔟𝔩𝔦𝔬𝔤𝔯𝔞𝔭𝔥𝔦𝔞𝔫𝔞.

Annotated List of the various Publications,—Books, Reviews, Magazine and Newspaper Articles, &c.,—relating to the genius, works, and character of GEORGE CRUIKSHANK, which appeared during his Life ; the Pamphlets, Letters to the "Times," &c., written by himself ;—and the Leading Articles, Lectures, Notices Critical and Obituary, and miscellaneous Essays, occasioned by his Death.

———

(1) DURING HIS LIFE.

Blackwood's Magazine, July 1823. "Lectures on the Fine Arts, No. 1. On George Cruikshank," attributed variously to J. G. Lockhart and Professor Wilson—has special reference to the "Points of Humour."

———

is as happy as the thought, and where the student of etching may find models, as the student of manners finds a record, or a suggestion. In etchings of this class CRUIKSHANK carries one great virtue of the art to perfection—its simple frankness. He is so direct and unaffected that only those who know the difficulties of etching can appreciate the power that lies behind his unpretending skill ; there is never, in his most admirable plates, the trace of a vain effort."—*Etching and Etchers,* 1876.

* I use this word advisedly, in its more extensive sense ; I do not forget that Mr. Watts Phillips was a *pupil* of the artist.

† "All the real masters of caricature deserve honour in this respect, that their gift is peculiarly their own,—innate and incommunicable. No teaching, no hard study, will ever enable other people to equal, in their several ways, the works of LEECH and CRUIKSHANK ; whereas, the power of pure drawing is communicable, within certain limits, to every one who has good sight and industry. I do not, indeed, know how far, by devoting the attention to points of character, caricaturist-skill may be laboriously attained ; but certainly the power is, in the masters of the school, innate from their childhood."
"Taken, all in all, the works of CRUIKSHANK have the most sterling value of any belonging to this class produced in England."   —Ruskin's *Modern Painters,* vol. iv., p. 377.

‡ BYRON. "Monody on the Death of Sheridan."

The town was just then running mad after the *Life in London,* and the critic, dazzled by the effulgence of that literary comet, bursts into a fine strain of eulogy :—

> " But what a start did he make when his genius had received a truer and diviner impulse from the splendid imagination of an Egan ! How completely, how *toto cœlo,* did he out-Cruikshank himself when he was called upon to embody the conceptions of that remarkable man in the designs for ' Tom and Jerry ' ? The world felt this, and he felt it himself."

Aspersions Answered : an Explanatory Statement addressed to the Public at Large, and to every Reader of the *Quarterly Review* in particular. By William Hone, 1824, 8vo.

> Contains the interesting passage relating to G. C., quoted in the present essay, page 18.

Blackwood's Magazine, Feb. 1824. "Lectures on the Fine Arts, No. 2. On Henry Alken and others,"—with, incidentally, some important remarks on G. C.

Somerset House Gazette and Literary Museum, or Weekly Miscellany of Fine Arts, Antiquities, and Literary Chit-Chat. Edited by Ephraim Hardcastle (W. H. Pyne, the Artist), London, 1824, 2 vols, 4to.

> Review of Cruikshank's *Points of Humour.* After speaking of Gillray,— "that extraordinary genius, the prince of caricaturists, the inventor of pictorial burlesques,"—the critic goes on to say :—
>
> > " The original style is, we repeat, the invention of Gillray ; its application, and what the clever genius in question has superadded, is the next point for consideration. We will roundly assert, then, that George Cruikshank has proved himself worthy of stepping into his witty predecessor's shoes, and wonderously as they have been worn, they fit as though he had been measured for them. They are yet as strong, and well to wear, and everything but new. * * * *
> >
> > " In this little volume of *little* plates, he has established his reputation as a great master ; and if we might be allowed to *coin* a title for his *copper,* we should designate them 'Gems of Humour.' We admire the beautiful and spirited needles of ' Della Bella ' and ' Callott ' (*sic*); the truth and unaffected style of Hollar's *point,* and the taste of many other famous *etchers* we could name, but certainly none but the unique *point* of George Cruikshank ever incorporated the workings of passion and expression in the human visage on the diminutive size of a millet seed.
> >
> > " We neglected to notice that spirited scrap, the *Downfall of the Church,* in the first part of the work in question. It is the happiest effort of the masterly art of etching in small, ancient or modern, that we could name. To those unacquainted with connoisseurship in these matters, we shall refer them to this plate as an example of the clearness and brilliancy of the execution, when the operation of *biting* the line is successfully performed. * * * We must repeat that these pointed emanations of his prolific point are unique gems of humour." vol. 1., p. 365.

The Cigar ; by Ebenezer Cullchickweed. London, 12mo, (N.D.)

> This witty and amusing volume of tales and anecdotes was really written by William Clarke to whom allusion is made at page 44 of the present essay. It originally appeared about 1825; but my edition is a more recent issue,—a fat little volume of nearly 500 pages, without date. It contains, (p. 426), a short article on G. C. as THE YOUNG HOGARTH.

Blackwood's Magazine, June 1827, vol. xxvii.

> A discursive rhapsodical article by Professor Wilson on the *Illustrations of Time,* praising the artist, dealing Jem Ward a "facer," attacking Shakespeare's Witches, Ghosts and Fairies, lauding the *Magazine,* and winding up with an invitation to George Cruikshank to pay a visit to Edinburgh, and become "one of the *Noctes Ambrosianœ,*"—which being interpreted means " The Ambrosian Knights." Reprinted in *The Works of John Wilson,* 1856, (" Essays Critical and Imaginative,") vol. v., pp. 128-157.

Hone's Every Day Book, 1827, 8vo.   Article on Phrenological Illustrations,—
   vol. 2, p. 1821.

Each plate is separately characterized through seven columns of text ;
and the article winds up with the following remarks upon the artist :—

> " His inimitable powers have hitherto entertained and delighted the public far
> more to the emolument of others than himself ; and now that he has ventured to
> ' take a benefit ' on his own account, there cannot be a doubt that his admirers
> will encourage their ' old favorite ' to successive endeavours for their amusement
> and instruction.   His entire talents have never been called forth ; and some are of
> a far higher order than even the warmest friends to his pencil can conceive."

In the former volume of the *Every Day Book* (I, 903), is a spirited sketch
of "The London Barrow Woman," an obsolete street trader, cut on wood
by Henry White.   Of this Hone says :—

> "Mr. George Cruikshank, whose pencil is distinguished by power of decision
> in every character he sketches, and whose close observation of passing manners is
> unrivalled by any artist of the day, has sketched the Barrow Woman for the *Every
> Day Book* from his own recollection of her, aided by my own."

The Every Night Book, or Life After Dark.   By the author of "The Cigar,"
   (William Clarke).   London, 1827, 8vo.

> Humorous vignette by G. C. on title-page ; contains the allusion to George
> Cruikshank cited on page 45 ; and the story about Moncrieff and his dramatization
> of "Tom and Jerry," referred to on page 37.

The Mirror of Literature, Amusement, and Instruction, London, 1828, 8vo,
   vol. xi., page 102.

> A four column review of *Punch and Judy*, in which, but for the statement that
> "his sketches are full of the *vis comica*," it might have been said that the part of
> the artist was left out.

Fraser's Magazine, June, 1830.   A Review of *Three Courses and a Dessert*,
   pp. 549-554.

> "We rejoice to see this eminent artist at last fairly emerged from the slough
> of politics, in which it was his original fate to be plunged.   His illustrations of
> Mr. Hone's pamphlets, which floated the lumber, for nothing was more dull or
> leaden than the dead bodies of the prose and verse to which they were tied, could
> not fail to be received with dislike or disgust by a class which acknowledged his
> merits, and would gladly have patronised his labours.   *   *   *   Ridiculing and
> caricaturing a husband, no matter what his rank may be, for endeavouring to get
> rid of a wife whose guilt was notorious, and whose conduct was disgraceful, were
> tasks that ought to be left to the herd who prostitute their pens and pencils for
> hire, and not to have formed the occupation of a man of genius.   It was work quite
> good enough for Hone ; but altogether unworthy of Cruikshank.
>   "He has now, however, shaken off the sable stains, and is enriching our
> language—we were about to say—with productions of Hogarthian humour.   In
> this path we are happy to know that the humour he is sure of obtaining, will
> not be barren.   Under the *patronage* of his former friends, his labours, which
> redeemed their dulness and put money into their purses, were almost unpaid.
> We have heard it said that the munificent remuneration he received from Hone
> amounted to eighteen pounds.   Such is too often the fate of genius when, with its
> characteristic improvidence, it suffers trading avarice to prey upon it."

*Pierce Egan's Finish to the Adventures of Tom, Jerry, and Logic, in their
   Pursuits through Life In and Out of London*, illustrated by the pencil of
   Robert Cruikshank.   London, 1830, 8vo.

> Several references to the brothers Cruikshank in Chapter I. ; and the state-
> ment of Moncrieff, the Dramatist, cited, with that half-and-half sort of demur
> which seems almost equivalent to assent, to the effect :—that "the characters of
> Tom, Jerry and Logic, were *auto*-biographical sketches of the artists to whom they
> originally severally owe their being.   The talented, spirited GEORGE CRUIKSHANK
> was himself, in all the better points, the spirited TOM he has so admirably

delineated ; his very clever brother ISAAC, then, perhaps, less experienced, condescended to pass for JERRY ; and the *downey* PIERCE (' none but himself can be his parallel ') was his own LOGIC. Having, *tria juncta in uno,* produced the admirable foundation of this Piece, may they speedily furnish the public with some more of their Larks, Sprees, and Rambles—the world will thank them for the gift."—page 25.

Fraser's Magazine, August, 1833.

Notice by Maginn ; portrait by Maclise. Both reproduced in the *Maclise Gallery,* by William Bates. Chatto and Windus, 1874, 4to.

The Monthly Magazine.

Essay on Life, and Genius, with portrait and "illustrations of his talent at various periods of his career."

The Georgian Era ; Memoirs of the most Celebrated Persons, &c. London, 1834, 4 vols, 8vo.

Long notice of George Cruikshank, the "Prince of Humorous Designers," (vol. iv., p. 226), written probably by William Clarke, the editor, or Gilbert Abbott a' Becket, his coadjutor.

The Queen and the Union ! No Repeal ! No O'Connell !

An anti-repeal broadside, with forty-eight lines of text, signed "G. C." surmounted by a large emblematic wood-cut, representing O'Connell, striking with a hatchet, inscribed "Repeal," at the clasped hands of Britannia and Hibernia. Designed and published by George Cruikshank, sold by David Bogue, &c. Price threepence.—N. D., *circa* 1843.

The London and Westminster Review, August, 1838. Vol. xxxi., No. 2.

Essay on Wood-engraving, with illustrations, including two by G. C.

The Westminster Review, Aug., 1840.

Contains the celebrated illustrated article by W. M. Thackeray ; issued separately, "with additional etchings," by H. Hooper, Pall Mall, in the same year ; reprinted in the author's complete works, without the illustrations.

Portraits of Public Characters. By the Author of *Random Recollections, The Great Metropolis,* &c. London, 1841. 2 vols. 8vo.

The writer of this work,—James Grant,—has given us (Vol. II., pp. 236-257) a not altogether uninteresting account of the artist, the numerous absurdities and blunders in which are doubtless attributable to the strange principle on which he drew his "portraits,"—the studied absence of their prototypes. "In order," says he, "to write with greater freedom, fairness and fidelity, I have had no intercourse, while preparing the work, with any of the subjects of my sketches." A good-tempered and humorous exposure of the silly tittle-tattle contained in this paper, purporting to be from the pen of the Artist himself, and entitled "My Portrait," forms the leading paper in No. 1 of the *Omnibus.*

The Omnibus, No. I., 1841.

Contains the article referred to above entitled "My Portrait," purporting to be written by the artist, and accompanied by a finely-executed portrait of himself on steel.

The London Journal, Nov. 20, 1840.

Portrait, Biographical Notice, and Illustrations copied from the *Bottle* series.

Household Words, Aug. 23, 1851.

Contains an article by Charles Dickens entitled "Whole Hogs," referring to the *Fairy Library* of G. C., and the liberties taken with the time-hallowed Nursery stories.

Stop Thief! or Hints to Housekeepers to prevent Housebreaking.   By George
Cruikshank.   3rd ed., London (1851) 8vo.

Household Words, No. 184, Oct. 1, 1853.

> Contains the article " Frauds on the Fairies," written by Charles Dickens, in
> which the following passage occurs :
> " We have lately observed with pain the intrusion of a Whole Hog of un-
> wieldy dimensions into the fairy flower-garden. The rooting of the animal among
> the roses would in itself have awakened in us nothing but indignation ; our pain
> arises from his being violently driven in by a man of genius, our beloved friend,
> Mr. George Cruikshank. That incomparable artist is, of all men, the last who
> should lay his exquisite hand on fairy text. In his own art he understands it so
> perfectly, and illustrates it so beautifully, so humourously, so wisely, that he
> should never lay down his etching-needle to ' edit ' the Ogre, to whom with that
> little instrument he can render such extraordinary justice."

Neues Allgemeines Künstler Lexicon, von G. R. Nagler.   München, 1835–52,
22 vols., 8vo.

> Contains biographico-critical notice of G. C.

Poems.   By Matthew Arnold.   London, 1854, 8vo.

> Contains the Sonnett referred to, page 37 :—
>
> To George Cruikshank, Esq.,
> On Seeing for the First Time his Picture of "The Bottle,"
> in the Country.
>
> Artist, whose hand, with horror wing'd, hath torn
> From the rank life of towns this leaf : and flung
> The prodigy of full-blown crime among
> Valleys and men to middle fortune born,
> Not innocent, indeed, yet not forlorn :
> Say, what shall calm us, when such guests intrude,
> Like comets on the heavenly solitude ?
> Shall breathless glades, cheer'd by shy Dian's horn,
> Cold-bubbling springs or caves ? Not so ! The Soul
> Breasts her own griefs : and, urg'd too fiercely, says :
> " Why tremble ? True, the nobleness of man
> May be by man effaced : man can controul,
> To pain, to death, the bent of his own days,
> Know thou the worst. So much, not more, he *can.*"   p. 227.

Museum of Foreign Literature.   Philadelphia, 8vo, vol. V., p. 563.

> Contains Essay on genius of G. C.   I have not actually seen this.

George Cruikshank's Magazine.   Edited by " Frank Fairlegh " (Mr. Frank E.
Smedley).   London, D. Bogue, 1854.

> This venture survived through two numbers only ; but it is worthy to be
> specially mentioned here as containing (Feb. 1854) the Artist's defence of the
> liberties he had taken with Fairy Tales, in answer to the paper of Charles
> Dickens, " Frauds on the Fairies," in *Household Words,* referred to in a preceding
> article.

The Glass and the New Crystal Palace.   By George Cruikshank.   With cuts.
London, 1853, 8vo.

> Interesting from its personal details. After relating how he came to be a
> Teetotaler, George adds :—" I used to smoke, and clung to that contemptible,
> stupid and dirty habit for three years after I had left off wine and beer, and
> stopped my grog. I had been reasoning with myself for years against this silly
> and injurious bad habit of smoking ; but at last I laid down my meerschaum pipe,
> and said, lie you there ! and I will never take you up again,—and I never have,—
> nor never will. As I had been *an inveterate smoker for upwards of thirty years,* it
> shows that this habit may be broken as well as the pipe."   p. 21.

The Illustrated London Magazine : a monthly Journal of Literature and Art. Vol. V. Oct. and Nov., 1855. (Ward, Locke and Co.)

> Contains a paper entitled "Art and Humour; No. I., GEORGE CRUIKSHANK,' illustrated by 15 wood-cut designs chiefly from *Mornings in Bow Street;* and a Review of the *True Legend of St. Dunstan,* with three illustrations by G. C. from that work. The following passage is worth preservation :—
>
> "Copies of the works of this artist, from first to last, would fill a couple of waggons. No one, not even himself, has a perfect collection ; but an imperfect one, of a great Cruikshank collector of our acquaintance, not containing a *tenth* of his works, fills eight large elephant volumes ; that is, the woodcuts and plates are mounted to that size, eight or so of them on a sheet ! Not one of these plates, also, but has its beauties ; not one of them but is full of patient thought, kindly, honest purpose, and thorough good feeling. To look over them would astonish our readers, and make them feel gratitude and wonder ; wonder at such unceasing thought, such unwearied industry ; gratitude for the thousand pleasant and kindly fancies ; the hundred hints, advice, merry quips, and cranks, and turns, which have been given to this work-a-day world by an artist's pencil ; and, let us add, by which it has, day by day, from the old times of 'Tom and Jerry,' been humanised and reformed." p. 279.

Men of the Time: Biographical Sketches of Eminent Living Characters. London, 1856, 8vo.

> Long biographical notice of G. C. See also later editions.

A Slice of Bread and Butter cut by George Cruikshank, being the Substance of a Speech, &c. London, 1857, 8vo.

Cambridge School of Art: Inaugural Soirée. Mr. Ruskin's Address, and Reports of the Speeches of S. Redgrave, R.A., and Mr. George Cruikshank, with a full account of the Proceedings of the Evening. Cambridge, 1858, 16mo.

Old Faces in New Masks. By Robert Blakey, Ph. D. London, 1859, 8vo.

> Contains, besides the admirable etched front, and title by G. C., an essay, "Historical Sketch of British Caricature," (pp. 164—205) in which a short but laudatory mention of the artist occurs.

Elements of Drawings in Three Letters to Beginners, by John Ruskin, A.M., 1860, 8vo.

> "If you ever happen to meet with the two volumes of *Grimm's German Stories,* which were illustrated by him (G. C.) long ago, pounce upon them instantly : the etchings in them are the finest things, next Rembrandt's, that, as far as I know, have been done since etching was invented You cannot work at them too much, nor copy them too often," &c. p. 350.

British Artists, from Hogarth to Turner, &c. By Walter Thornbury, 2 vols. London, 1861, 8vo.

> Contains a long and admirable article on "The English Caricaturists and King Cruikshank."

A Pop-Gun fired off by George Cruikshank in Defence of the British Volunteers of 1803, against the uncivil attack upon that body by General W. Napier. With observations on our National Defence, Self-Defence, &c. London, 8vo. (1860.)

> Contains eight wood-cuts from designs by the author, including two portraits of himself.

The Weekly Record, Nov. 29, 1862.

>Catalogue of Pictures, Sketches, &c., in "The George Cruikshank Gallery."

Blackwood's Magazine, August, 1863.

>Contains an excellent article on G. C.; with incidental remarks on Gillray and Doyle.

The Autographic Mirror, Dec. 15, 1864.

>Fac-simile of holograph letter from G. C. to William Hayward relative to etchings for the *Comic Almanack,* and Thackeray's essay in the *Westminster,*—with some fac-simile pencillings.

The Worship of Bacchus. A critique by John Stewart; a Descriptive Lecture by George Cruikshank; and Opinions of the Press. London, 1863, 8vo., pp. 24.

>In justice to the artist, I would here remind the reader that this picture,—or rather coloured cartoon,—which has provoked so much adverse criticism, should be regarded as a *sketch,* rather than as a perfected work of art. In a letter to myself now before me, Oct. 11, 1876. he states that "it was never perfectly finished;" and regrets this the more, as it is "contrary to the laws of the National Gallery to allow an artist to touch his work after it is once in the possession of the authorities." There was a long article on the picture, about this period, in *Chambers's Journal.*
>
>Goldsmith, in his well-known epitaphian verses on Ned Purdon, has well indicated the miseries of the "booksellers' hack" of his day. I hardly know that matters have much changed for the better in our own time; and the luckless wight, whether author or artist, who has to seek the intermediary aid of the publisher, will find,—some few exceptions apart,—that, metaphorically speaking, he gets as many kicks as halfpence. That George Cruikshank was, all his life, in this position, is the great secret of his failure to accumulate wealth; and so convinced was he,—as he expressed in conversation shortly before his death,—after an experience of nearly three quarters of a century, of the inevitability of this result, that, if he had to begin his career again, he said, it would be the *painting-brush,* and not the *etching-needle* which should express his inventions; and he would have done altogether with the middlemen, who had, in all their mutual transactions, managed to "swallow the oyster and leave him the shells."
>
>The veteran artist farther asserted that the most profitable jobs Gillray, Rowlandson, and he himself had met with in their working careers, were what he termed, the "washing of other people's dirty linen,"—by which he meant the putting on to copper the crude designs of fashionable amateurs. Such jobs were quickly executed, and liberally paid for; and the artists regarded them, to use the words of a valued correspondent to whom I am indebted for the statement, as "so much 'fat,'—a sort of Caanan in the wilderness."

Love's Last Labour Not Lost. By George Daniel. London, Pickering, 1863, 8vo.

>Only 250 copies were printed of this interesting little volume, which contains (p. 163) an appreciative and feeling tribute to the memory of the author's old friend and literary associate, ROBERT CRUIKSHANK.

A Catalogue of a Selection from the Works of George Cruikshank, extending over a period of upwards of Sixty Years, from 1799 to 1863. London, 1863, 4to.

>The objects exhibited at Exeter Hall in 1863 are described as consisting of "upwards of one hundred oil-paintings, water-colour drawings, and original sketches, together with over a thousand proof etchings from popular works, caricatures, scrap-books, song-headings, &c., and the 'Worship of Bacchus.'" There is a short preface to the Catalogue by the Artist himself, in which he says:—"The 'George Cruikshank Gallery,' as it is called, originated in consequence of many persons having expressed their belief that G. C., the caricaturist of former days, was the grandfather of the person who produced the 'Worship of Bacchus.' The Committee, therefore, who are exhibiting 'the Worship of Bacchus' requested to have some of my early works, in order to show that they were the production of one and the same person; or to prove, in fact, that I am not my own grandfather."

A Discovery concerning Ghosts, with a Rap at the " Spirit Rappers," by George
   Cruikshank. *Illustrated with Cuts ; to which is added a few Parting
   Raps at the " Rappers," with Questions, Suggestions and Advice to the
   Davenport Brothers, Dedicated to the Ghost Club. Price One Shilling.
   London, 1864.* Royal 8vo, pp. 60.

> Second edition, with 10 woodcuts. . The former edition appeared in the pre-
> ceding year.

Once a Week, Sept. 30, 1865.

> A paper on "Caricature," by C. D. Y. (pp. 409–414), with incidental remarks
> upon G. C.

Dictionnaire Universel des Contemporains, &c. Par G. Vapereau. Troisième
   édition. Paris, 1865, 8vo.

> We may learn from a foreigner even something concerning George Cruikshank
> with which we were previously unacquainted :—"La collection du *Punch*, et celle
> du *Comic Almanack*, dout il fut le constant collaborateur fournissent aussi de
> nombreuses preuves de son talent pour la caricature." It is generally believed in
> his own country that he never made a single design for *Punch.*

A Treatise on Wood Engraving, Historical and Practical, by John Jackson
   and W. A. Chatto. Second edition. London (Bohn), 1866, 8vo.

> A short notice of G. C. (p. 595*), with four illustrations by him, and one by
> his brother Robert.

Essays on Art, by Francis Turner Palgrave. London, 1866, 8vo.

> Contains article on "The Cruikshank Exhibition," July, 1863.

Fine Art, chiefly contemporary ; Notices reprinted with Revisions. By William
   Michael Rossetti. London, 1867, 8vo.

> Contains article on "The Exhibition of Cruikshank's Collected Works," 1862.

Caricature History of the Georges, or Annals of the House of Hanover, &c.
   By Thomas Wright, F.S.A. London, 8vo. (1868)

> "Cruikshank was the great caricaturist of the period "—writes the author in
> his brief notice of the Regency lampoons. It may seem strange that no further
> allusion is made to the artist ; and it is from the "Preface" alone that we learn
> that the ground professedly covered by the History is that of the "Reigns of the
> Three Georges" only.

Etching and Etchers, by Philip Gilbert Hamerton. London, Macmillan,
   1868, 4to.

> "Cruikshank and Doyle," pp. 133–141. Second edition, 1876.

Les Merveilles de la Gravure, par George Duplessis. Paris, 1869, 8vo.

> "La Gravure en Angleterre, — l'école humoristique,' p. 244,—notices of
> Hogarth, Gillray, Rowlandson, and the Cruikshanks.

Memories of My Time, including Personal Reminiscences of Eminent Men.
   By George Hodder. London, 1870, 8vo.

> Notice of George Cruikshank, pp. 104–108.—"By a natural association of
> ideas,"—commences the Reminiscent,—"the name of GEORGE CRUIKSHANK seems
> to connect itself with that of KENNY MEADOWS, for there is not much difference in
> their ages, and both have spent the greater part of a long life in illustrating
> popular works by the exercise of an imaginative power which has always added
> strength and grace to the subject-matter they have undertaken to embody."

Life of Charles Dickens. By R. Shelton Mackenzie, LL.D. Philadelphia, 1870, 8vo.

> Here, among the reminiscences of the brothers Cruikshank, with whom the writer states he was intimate when in London, we have, reproduced, the claim of George to be the originator of most of the characters in *Oliver Twist.* This story, originally published by Dr. Mackenzie in the *Round Table*, a transatlantic serial, and copied in the biography of Dickens put forth by the late John Camden Hotten, is treated in Forster's *Life of Charles Dickens,* vol. I., p. 132, and the preliminary matter to vol. II.

Notes and Queries. March 19th, 1870.

> Contains a paper by Mr. J. C. Roger, giving an account of the piratical appropriation of some of G. C.'s designs in the *Illustrations of Time, &c.*, by the proprietor of *Bell's Life in London,* and the artist's inability to obtain redress.

Remarks on Education by George Cruikshank, with a Slice of Bread and Butter on the same subject. London, 1870, 8vo., pp. 16.

> Contains three wood-cuts after G. C.

Universal Catalogue of Books on Art, &c., published by the Science and Art Department of the Committee of Council on Education, South Kensington. "First Proofs." London, 1870, 2 vols. 4to.

> A bibliography of George Cruikshank describing about 120 separate pieces.

The Period. Sept. 17, 1870.

> Article and coloured caricature-portrait of George Cruikshank riding a Hobby-horse, as "The Champion of Temperance."

Notes and Queries. Nov. 12, 1870, and Jan. 14, 1871.

> Account of G. C.'s illustrations for *Roscoe's Novelist's Library.*

A Descriptive Catalogue of the Works of George Cruikshank, Etchings, Wood-cuts, Lithographs, Glyphographs, &c. With a list of Books illustrated by him. By George William Reid, Keeper of the Prints and Drawings in the British Museum. With an *Essay on his Genius and Works*, by Edward Bell, M.A., and three hundred and thirteen illustrations on India paper. London, 1871, 4to, Bell and Daldy.

> Of this sumptuous work the impression was limited to 135 copies, and one of these is worth now a dozen guineas at least. Of the designs recorded, 2657 are Etchings, 1693 are Wood-cuts, 72 are Glyphographs, and 60 are Lithographs; while the books, pamphlets, broadsides, &c., described amount to nearly 400.

Essay on the Genius and Character of George Cruikshank. By R. Shelton Mackenzie, LL.D.

> Published in America. Dr. Mackenzie will be remembered as once resident in Birmingham, and connected with the local press of that town. He is author of *Titian,* a novel, 3 vols., 8vo., &c.

The Illustrated Review. No. XXX. January 1st, 1872.

> Contains portrait and illustrations.

The Portfolio: An Artistic Periodical. Edited by Philip Gilbert Hamerton.

> Contains a critical article on G. C., by F. G. Stephens, with an illustration.

The Artist and the Author : A Statement of Facts. By the Artist, George
Cruikshank. London (1872), Bell and Daldy. 8vo. pp. 16.

> The object of this pamphlet is to set forth the artist's claim to have been
> "the originator" of certain of the novels of Charles Dickens and W. Harrison
> Ainsworth.

Pro and Con. March, April, and May, 1873.

> Portrait and illustrations.

The London Figaro. Oct. 1, 1873.

> Contains a paper entitled "OUR GEORGE," in the series of the so-called
> "Parnassian Portrait Gallery."

The Illustrated Review. London, 1873-4.

> Contains a valuable series of papers "Caricature Past and Present," by Mr.
> Joseph Grego, on Gillray, Bunbury, Isaac Cruikshank, &c. The articles, which
> extend over a period of six months, are copiously illustrated; and the one on Gillray
> forms a sort of introduction to the large and exhaustive essay on that "Prince
> of Caricaturists," from the same pen, published in Dec. 1873, by Chatto and
> Windus, with the name of the late Thomas Wright, M.A., upon the title-page, as
> "Editor." These papers have been translated into French.

*English Graphic Satire, and its relation to different styles of Painting,
Sculpture, and Engraving : a Contribution to the History of the English
School of Art.* The numerous illustrations selected and drawn from the
originals by Robert William Buss, painter, designer, and etcher, and
reproduced by photo-lithography. Printed for the author by Virtue and
Co. for private circulation only, 1874. 4to. pp. XX. and 195.

> It is much to be regretted that this able contribution to the history of
> caricature is not more generally accessible to the public.

A Gallery of Illustrious Literary Characters (1830–1838), drawn by the late
Daniel Maclise, R.A., and accompanied by Notices chiefly by the late
William Maginn, LL.D. Edited by William Bates, B.A., &c. London,
Chatto and Windus, 1874, 4to.

> Contains Maclise's portrait, and Maginn's notice from *Fraser's Magazine;* long
> "Note" by the Editor, pp. 106–109; and supplementary "Note" on the "Cruik-
> shank Testimonial," p. 227.

*A Dictionary of the Artists of the English School, Painters, Sculptors, Archi·
tects, Engravers, and Ornamentists, &c.* By Samuel Redgrave. London,
1874, 8vo.

The Bookseller. Christmas number, 1875.

> Contains essay on the works of G. C., with illustrations.

The Daily Telegraph, July 5th, 1875.

> Contains article on G. C. and his work.

L' Art. Revue Hebdomadaire Illustrée. Deuxième année, tome III., p. 144, 1876.

> A notice of George Cruikshank's works as exhibited at the Royal Westminster
> Aquarium.
> See also Tome II., 1875, p. 300. Tome III., pp. 277–304.

The Leisure Hour. Nov., 1875.

  A series of papers on the English Caricaturists, including, of course, G. C

L'Art. Revue Hebdomadaire Illustrée. Première année, 1875.

  Contains articles, " La Caricature Anglaise Contemporaine," par Victor Champier. For special reference to G. C. see tome Ier. pp. 291-6.

A History of Caricature and Grotesque in Literature and Art. By Thomas Wright, M,A., F.S.A. With numerous illustrations drawn and engraved by F. W. Fairholt, F.S.A. London, 1865, 4to.

  This able and interesting work, which winds up with an eulogy upon the genius and character of G. C., was translated into French by Amédée Pichot. (Paris, 1875, 8vo.)

The Daily Telegraph. Aug. 7, 1876.

  Leading article on George Cruikshank as an Etcher and a Draughtsman on Wood, doubtless by Mr. G. A. Sala.

Eighty-two Illustrations on Steel, Stone, and Wood, by George Cruikshank, with letter-press descriptions. 4to, N.D.

  Contains designs which had previously appeared in various books issued by the publisher, William Tegg.

The West Middlesex Advertiser. January 19th, 1878.

Catalogue of a Selection from the Works of George Cruikshank, Esq. Produced from 1799 to 1875 ; consisting of upwards of one hundred Oil Paintings, Water Colour Drawings, and Original Sketches. Together with over a thousand Proof Etchings, &c. The Property of the Royal Aquarium Society. London, 1877, 8vo., pp. 22.

---

(2) AFTER HIS DEATH.

The Times. February 2, 1878.

  Leading article, probably written by Tom Taylor, M.A., concluding with the following remarks :—" What CRUIKSHANK has left behind him—and it is enormous in amount, and wonderfully various in quality—contains much that will, if we are not mistaken, secure him a place in the artistic history of his country, next to HOGARTH, and not far behind him. * * * There is not a single beautiful face or figure, probably, in the whole range of CRUIKSHANK's work. But nowhere in it is there anything base, anything loose, anything in the largest sense of the word immoral. It is something remarkable that a satirist who chastised fashionable and popular vice for more than sixty years almost without intermission, should have left not one drawing behind him that might not be handed round in the family circle of any English household. In this respect, at least, CRUIKSHANK might claim to be superior to HOGARTH, and his inferiority in other respects is not so signal that they may not be named together as the two greatest caricaturists that England has produced."

The Daily News. Feb. 2, 1878.

  Leading article.

The Birmingham Daily Mail. Feb. 2, 1878.

  Leading article.

The Daily Telegraph. Feb. 4, 1878.

  Leading article by Mr. G. A. Sala.

The Standard.   Feb. 4, 1878.

      Leading article.

The Globe.   Feb. 4, 1878.

      Long leading article in which the following remarks occur : " ———— That he was essentially an artist of original genius is beyond question. There have been, and there are, many men more completely masters of their art in all technical knowledge and skill, but we know of none, either English or foreign, more richly endowed with the faculty of invention, with a more genuine sense of humour, or with a power of conveying his meaning with more incisive clearness, &c."

The Christian Herald.   Feb. 6, 1878.

      Portrait and article.

The Temperance Record.   Feb. 7, 1878.

      Article and extracts.

The Christian Globe.   Feb. 7, 1878.

      Portrait and article.

The Athenæum.   Feb. 9, 1878.

      Long obituary article, from which I extract the following remarks :—" He was a pure satirist of the richest vein, inexhaustible in invention, incomparably dramatic, often profoundly pathetic, and, in those tender passages which it was his delight to portray, he often stirred us in an unexampled fashion. As an artist *per se* his rank ought to be higher than that popularly awarded to him, for, some defects of taste apart, defects which were mostly due to the influence of the age in which he was born, he always drew with admirable fidelity, precision and felicity, &c."

The Academy.   Feb. 9, 1878.

      Long obituary article by Mr. W. B. Scott.

The Saturday Review.   Feb. 9, 1878.

      Obituary article.

The Builder.   Feb. 9, 1878.

      Obituary article.

Punch.   Feb. 9, 1878.

      " England is the poorer by what she can ill spare—a man of genius. Good, kind, genial, honest, and enthusiastic GEORGE CRUIKSHANK, whose frame appeared to have lost so little of its wiry strength and activity, whose brain seemed as full of fire and vitality at four-score as at forty, has passed away quietly and painlessly after a few days' struggle. He never worked for *Punch*, but he always worked with him, putting his unresting brain, his skill - in some forms of Art unrivalled—and his ever productive fancy, at the service of humanity and progress, good works and good-will to man. His object, like our own, was always to drive home truth and urge on improvement by the powerful forces of fun and humour, clothed in forms sometimes powerful, sometimes grotesque, but never sullied by a foul thought, and ever dignified by a wholesome purpose.

      " His four-score and six years of life have been years of unintermitting labour, that was yet, always, labour of love. There never was a purer, simpler, more straightforward, or altogether more blameless man. His nature had something child-like in its transparency. You saw through him completely. There was neither wish nor effort to disguise his self-complacency, his high appreciation of himself, his delight in the appreciation of others, any more than there was to make himself out better, or cleverer, or more unselfish than his neighbours.

      " In him England has lost one who was, in every sense, as true a man as he was a rare and original genius, and a pioneer in the arts of illustration. It is gratifying to see the tributes of hearty recognition his death has called forth. It is a duty on *Punch's* part, as a soldier in the same army in which GEORGE CRUIKSHANK held such high rank so long, to add his wreath to the number already laid upon this brave old captain's grave."

Notes and Queries.   Feb. 9, 1878.

Interesting reminiscences of the deceased artist by Mr. H. S. Ashbee, F.S.A. who relates the following characteristic anecdote :—" Cruikshank was happy, to the very last, in the possession of both mental and physical activity. He was a man of progress ; he went with the times, and had sympathy with the young generation springing up around him. He eagerly joined the Volunteers, and became a leading figure in the movement. In early life he had been destined for the sea, and only escaped being sent on board a man-of-war (those were the times of the press-gang) by hiding away. When mentioning to me once that episode in his life, which must have changed his whole career, and deprived the world (as I then suggested to him) of such a fund of amusement and instruction—'Well,' answered Cruikshank, with a simplicity that was one of the great charms of his conversation, 'well, I should have done my duty, and become an admiral.'"

The Graphic.   Feb. 9, 1878.

Article by Miss Grace Stebbing.

The Illustrated Sporting and Dramatic News.   Feb. 9, 1878.

Long article, and portrait from the " Maclise Gallery."

Reynolds's Newspaper.   Feb. 10, 1878.

Short notice.

Land and Water.   Feb. 9, 1878.

A column of gossip on G. C., by a septuagenarian.

The Week.   Feb. 9, 1878.

Obituary notice—two columns :—" We cannot conclude these remarks with more fitting praise than by saying that at the end of a long and busy and laborious life as an artist, and forced, as he was, to deal largely with the fashionable vices of the last two—may we not say nearly three?—generations, he was one of those chosen few caricaturists who could boast that they had never pencilled a single drawing which an English mother would hesitate for a moment to place under the eyes of her daughter."

The Daily Telegraph.   Feb. 11, 1878.

Account of the funeral.

Mayfair.   Feb. 12, 1878.

Article—column and a half,—with caricature portrait of G. C. as pall-bearer at the funeral of Andrew Halliday. The following reminiscences merit preservation :—" Every anecdote concerning Mr. Cruikshank's personal career—and they are legion—is more or less connected with total abstinence in its 'muscular' phase. The story is told how the painter, in his quality of colonel of a regiment of volunteers, once set out with three oranges in his pocket, one of which he brought home at night, and how, towards the close of the field-day, he taunted the exhausted soldiers, who had freely imbibed, with an exulting reference to his own abstinence and consequent freshness. Most of the daily papers have mentioned Mr. Cruikshank's prowess in capturing, at the age of seventy or more, a desperate burglar But the most characteristic part of the story has, as far as we are aware, been omitted. While keeping a firm grasp of the thief with his left hand, the doughty little painter felt his own pulse with the other, and, finding that the accustomed 75 beats to the minute had not been increased by a single one in spite of exertion and excitement, he gravely began to enlarge upon the benefits of temperance, comparing his own calm with the thief's panting condition. That the rogue was also a drunkard he assumed as a matter of course. In this strange condition the pair were found by the policeman."

Fun.   Feb. 13, 1878.

ontains the following memorial stanzas :—

GEORGE CRUIKSHANK.

" While in unholy war foe strives with foe,
   Dead lies the hero of a great crusade ;
The pale-faced warr'or lays our hero low,
   Whose mighty weapon aye for right was swayed.

> "Vice fled before it, Falsehood bowed its head ;
> Injustice, cowed, turned on its recreant heel ;
> While the fierce light of honest Truth was shed
> In dazzling rays from his all-glorious steel.
>
> The pen is mightier than the sword, they say ;—
> Let both for once to his grand pencil yield ;
> Look back upon the foes in grim array
> His pencil left heart-pierced upon the field !
> It tore the victim from Death's vengeful grasp,
> It fought with vice in many a secret den ;
> The old knight falls, his weapon in his clasp,
> And leaves its work his monument to men."

The London Figaro.　Feb. 13, 20, 27, March 6, 13, 1878.

A series of papers, entitled, "Personal Recollections of George Cruikshank," from the pen of "Cuthbert Bede" (The Rev. E. Bradley.)

George Cruikshank : Artist, Humorist, Moralist. With several illustrations. Published by John Bursill, 36, Kennington Road, London.　Price twopence, 1878, 8vo, p. 16.

On the cover is an **announcement** addressed, " To Temperance Literary Societies, &c.," informing them that " Mr. J. Francis Bursill is prepared to give his highly-instructive and interesting Lecture, entitled, 'George Cruikshank : Artist, Humorist, and Temperance Reformer ; his Life and Labours ;' illustrated by a beautiful series of dissolving views, specially prepared for MR. BURSILL, being principally photographs, coloured and plain, from G. CRUIKSHANK'S works. In this Mr. Bursill has been assisted by several eminent collectors and publishers, and the collection of photographic transparencies used to illustrate this lecture is quite unique, embracing the entire career of the great artist."

L'Art.　Revue Hebdomadaire Illustrée.　Quatrième année.　Tome I., page 168, 1878.

Necrology of the artist, in which the following remarks occur :—" Le métier du père a été le point de départ du talent du fils qui, sans instruction première, sans éducation esthétique, mais grâce à une production constante, grâce à un esprit alerte, original, humoristique, flairant le goût du jour, suivant l'actualité tant littéraire que politique, en a fait un art véritable, bien que de second plan, et tiré une célébrité surabondamment justifiée par soixante-quinze aus de pratique et de succés.　Nen senlement GEORGE CRUIKSHANK fut un physionomie, une personnalité, mais son œuvre est étroitement liée à la vie anglaise depuis le commencement de ce siècle si bien qu' un critique peut écrire aujourdhui, sans trop d'exaggération, que, sans lui, cette vie semble désormais impossible."

Illustrated London News.　Feb. 16, 1878.

Portrait of G. C. and obituary notice, in which the following remarks occur :—" It is indeed possible that, if his early training and employment had been conversant with forms of beauty, grace, and majesty, instead of the uncouth and whimsical ugliness belonging to the caricature style, Cruikshank might have been the Turner of figure-painting—as it were the Shakspeare of that branch of art—displaying the widest range of conception and expression in his portraiture of diverse humours, and of the various passions and affections of the mind.　He might, at any rate, have been so qualified as to rival Hogarth, the most Shakspearian of all our painters ; but caricature and grotesque invention, which almost wholly engrossed the youth and prime manhood of our gifted contemporary, left his mind and hand no leisure for representing noble types and worthy aspects of human character, &c."

In the same number, Mr. G. A. Sala gives in his " Echoes of the Week " a short account of the burial of the artist in Kensal Green Cemetery, to which the following extract from the newspapers of Dec., 1878, will serve as supplement :—

"————The remains of the late George Cruikshank have been removed from their temporary resting place in Kensal Green Cemetery, and deposited in their final resting place in St. Paul's Cathedral.　In compliance with a generally expressed public wish, the Dean of St. Paul's gave his consent to the burial in the Cathedral, but as the Crypt was under repairs, the reception of the remains was deferred until last week.　The ceremony was of the simplest kind."

The Publishers' Circular.   Feb. 16, 1878.

Obituary notice :—" To omit the name of George Cruikshank from the history of England in the nineteenth century would be to leave out an essential factor from the story of the passions, merriments and moods of the people. Unhappily we have now to chronicle his death, and, although he died at the age of eighty-six, he was so full of vitality and vigour that his departure seems sudden and untimely. It was but a few days ago that, meeting Mr. R. H. Horne at the house of Mr. Bentley, the publisher, the veteran artist and colonel of volunteers, like Johnny Armstrong, ' danced a spring,' or rather, footed the difficult and rapid shuffle of the hornpipe, to show that there was yet life in him. * * * Cruikshank was entirely a draughtsman *per se* of exulting strength, value, honesty, purity, industry, and worth. He was a John Bull caricaturist of a now lost race ; a man of a true, noble, virtuous, and not over well-paid life, who has done the nation sound service, and of whom it may well be proud."

Chambers's Journal.   March 16, 1878.

Long article, " The Story of George Cruikshank."

The Weekly Welcome.   March 30, 1878.

Portrait and article.

Notes and Queries.   April 18, 1878.

Reminiscences of G. C. and his " Magazine "—six column article by "Cuthbert Bede" (Rev. E. Bradley).

The Leisure Hour.   April 27, 1878.

Fine portrait of G. C., accompanied by a long and interesting article, which closes with the following remarks :—" In appearance Cruikshank was no ordinary person. He was rather under the middle size, of graceful build, and firm muscular figure. His features were strikingly expressive,—an eye that looked you through, a nose rather of the Roman type, a mouth and lips of classical mould, and a capacious forehead, the whole countenance in middle life rather wildly set in a redundance of hair. He was constitutionally courageous, and being highly impulsive, was quickly stirred to action. Always prompt to take the initiative, whatever his hand found to do, he did it with all his might, not at all like your ultra-deliberate man who hesitate and hesitate, deterred by this difficulty and that, until the opportunity for action is past. His facile fingers were ever in the forelock of Time, grasping with a determined hold the as yet undeveloped events, and pressing them into his service. Hence the astonishing number and variety of his works, which will be hoarded and cherished long after the events and circumstances which gave rise to them have passed into oblivion. The last of England's purely satirical designers, he will be assuredly regarded as the greatest."

Notes and Queries.   June 1, 1878.

An interesting communication from Mr. J. Potter Briscoe, F.R.H.S., with extracts from a letter to him from G. C. relating to his illustrations to *Paradise Lost.* See page 48 of the present essay.

George Cruikshank, Artist and Humourist, with numerous Illustrations and a £1 Bank Note. By Walter Hamilton, F.R.G.S.   London, Eliot Stock.   Feb., 1878, 8vo., pp. 64.

Reprint, with additions, of a lecture read before the Chelsea Literary and Scientific Institution. Contains reproduction of the portrait from *The Omnibus,* and many wood-cuts.

The Bookseller.   March 2, 1878.

The Bookseller.   April 3, 1878.

The last two articles contain a chronological bibliography of the books illustrated by George Cruikshank, which, though not quite free from errors, will be found to convey much interesting information.

The Temple Bar Magazine.   April, 1878.

Article by Mr. Frederick Wedmore.

The Gentleman's Magazine. May, 1878.
> Article, "George Cruikshank ; a Life Memory," by George Augustus Sala.

Notes and Queries. May 26, 1878.
> A note by "Olphar Hamst," (Mr. Ralph Thomas) on G. C.'s library, and its recent sale by Sotheby, Wilkinson and Hodge.

Notes and Queries. June 15, 1878.
> A letter from Mr. William Tegg, the eminent publisher, about *Mirth and Morality*, illustrated by G. C.

The Art Journal. May, 1878.
> Obituary notice.

Scribner's Monthly. June, 1878. (A Transatlantic serial).
> Article on George Cruikshank, with twenty-three illustrations.

George Cruikshank: The Artist, the Humourist, and the Man. A Critico-Bibliographical Essay by William Bates, B.A., &c. With numerous illustrations, of which some are from original drawings never before engraved. Birmingham, Houghton and Hammond ; London, Houlston and Sons, 1878, 8vo., pp. 80. Price 1/-
> Of this Essay, 200 copies were struck off on large and thick paper, 4to, with the plates, of which many are additional, on India paper. Price 5/-

The same Work. Second edition, revised, with an additional section of "Bibliographiana," and several extra illustrations on India paper. Jan., 1879, 4to. Price 10/6.

Birmingham Daily Mail. Nov. 11, 1878.
> Long article on the above-mentioned Essay.

The Life of Rowlandson, the Caricaturist, with anecdotal descriptions of his Works and Times, and Sketches of his Contemporaries. (With numerous illustrations.) By Joseph Grego. Chatto and Windus, London, 1879, 4to.
> This important contribution to the history of caricature art is not yet before the public ; but by the kindness of the author I have enjoyed the privilege of perusing some of the proof-sheets, and place the book on record here as containing (pp. 15-19.) GEORGE CRUIKSHANK's opinion of his great predecessors or contemporaries. His admiration for GILLRAY,—" the greatest man, in his eyes who ever lived, indisputably 'the prince of caricaturists,' as he has appropriately christened him,"—was intense ; while he expressed the most enthusiastic appreciation of ROWLANDSON, not so much as a caricaturist as one might have thought, but as "an accomplished water-colour painter, the equal, as he considered, of most of the founders of our special school," and whose maritime sketches especially "recall in a forcible degree the drawings of WILLIAM VANDEVELDE who was, in Cruikshank's opinion, the only artist whose marine studies could be quoted in comparison.

------

(3) LETTERS WRITTEN BY GEORGE CRUIKSHANK,

AND PARAGRAPHS RELATING TO HIM AND HIS WORKS, IN THE "TIMES" NEWSPAPER, DURING THE LAST DECADE OF HIS LIFE.

1865, November 7. Page 12.
> Letter from G. C. on "Moderation in Drinking."

1866, April 6. Page 5.

    Letter from G. C. on " The Brighton Review."

868, January 4. Page 10

    Letter from G. C. on the formation of a Tempearnce Corps.

1868, July 17th. Page 10.

    Paragraph conveying G. C.'s request to the Editor to state that the "George Cruikshank, Junior, Artist" whose name had appeared in the Bankruptcy list of the preceding day, was a grandson of his brother Robert.

1870, January 29. Page 9.

    Letter from G. C. on the "National Education League."

1870, December 20. Page 9.

    Priced sale-list of Etchings and other Illustrations by G. C.

1871, December 30. Page 8.

    Letter from G. C. claiming to be the originator of *Oliver Twist.*

1872, April 8 ; Page 14. And April 11 ; Page 12.

    Letters on the origin of W. H. Ainsworth's *Miser's Daughter.*

1872, May 27. Page 14.

    A half-volume of text headed " A Shakespeare Gallery by George Cruikshank giving a laudatory critical account of the water-colour drawing, " The first appeance of William Shakespeare on the Stage of the Globe," produced by " the Nestor of Contemporary Art," and as then reproduced by the " Autotype Fine Art Company."

1872, December 28. Page 9.

    Letter from G. C., stating that certain illustrations which had recently appeared in *London Society* were not by him, but by "the son of his nephew, Percy Cruikshank"; and suggesting that, to avoid confusion, the latter should sign himself " G. Percy Cruikshank," instead of " George Cruikshank, Junior."

1873, May 31. Page 5.

    Letter from G. C. relating to his " Subscription Testimonial"; speaking of the serious loss which he had recently incurred from the forgery of a person with whom he had been induced to connect himself in an attempt to establish an Insurance Society for the Working Classes ; stating that his "efforts to serve his fellow-creatures" had cost him no less than £3,000, so that "the balance was on the wrong side"; and that, as for his Pensions, to which some allusion had been made, it would be a long time before they covered his losses.

1875, January 9. Page 7.

    Paragraph giving account of the republication of the " Bottle " series, in cheap form ; and the influence which it had had in abating Intemperance.

1875, June 28. Page 13.

    Paragraph giving account of the formation of a Committee to purchase from the Artist, for the Nation, a " complete Collection of his Works," produced during 76 years, consisting of 1,100 specimens, and which could be obtained from him for some £3,000.

1875, December 25. Page 7.

    Account of the purchase, for the " New Winter Garden, Westminster," of the large Cruikshank collection, " exhibited a few years since at Exeter Hall."

1876, August 3.   Page 9.

    Account of the Collection of the Works of G. C. at the " Royal Westminster Aquarium," as arranged by the Artist : about a third of a column.

1876, September 28.   Page 9.

    Letter from G. C. on "Street Accidents."

1877, June 22.   Page 4.

    Letter from G. C. on " Capital Punishment."

1877, December 6.   Page 10 : and December 19, page 9.

    Letters from G. C. asserting his claim to be the rightful designer of the Monument to Robert Bruce on the battle-field of Bannockburn ; and complaining of the treatment he had received.

1878, May 17.   Page 7.

    Account of the Sale of his Pictures and other personal effects.

1878, May 22.   Page 11.

    Statement that the Civil List Pension, enjoyed by the Artist, is to be continued to his Widow.

(From Original Pencil Drawing.)

FINIS.